Old Testament Narratives and Speech Act Theory

Old Testament Narratives and Speech Act Theory

Creating Worlds with Words

Steven T. Mann

LEXINGTON BOOKS

Lanham • Boulder • New York • London

Published by Lexington Books
An imprint of The Rowman & Littlefield Publishing Group, Inc.
4501 Forbes Boulevard, Suite 200, Lanham, Maryland 20706
www.rowman.com

86-90 Paul Street, London EC2A 4NE

British Library Cataloguing in Publication Information Available

Library of Congress Cataloging-in-Publication Data Available

Names: Mann, Steven Thatcher, author.
Title: Old Testament narratives and speech act theory : creating worlds with words /
    Steven T. Mann.
Description: Lanham : Lexington Books, [2025] | Includes bibliographical references
    and index. | Summary: "Old Testament Narratives and Speech Act Theory explores
    the ways in which words can create worlds within Old Testament narratives. Whereas
    characters can use their words in particular ways to impact the imaginations of their
    listeners, the storyteller attempts to transform the audience with the world(s) of the
    narrative"—Provided by publisher.
Identifiers: LCCN 2024048820 | ISBN 9781978716865 (cloth) |
    ISBN 9781978716872 (ebook)
Subjects: LCSH: Bible. Old Testament—Criticism, Narrative. | Speech acts (Linguistics) |
    Bible. Old Testament—Language, style.
Classification: LCC BS1182.3 .M366 2025 | DDC 221.6/6—dc23/eng/20241206
LC record available at https://lccn.loc.gov/2024048820

Contents

1 Speech Act Theory and Biblical Narrative   1

2 A Clash of Imaginations in Genesis 4   11

3 A Prayerful Imagination: The Power of "Perhaps"
(Gen. 18:16–33; Exod. 32:1–14; Amos 7:1–6)   29

4 Predatory and Protective Worlds in Exodus 1:8–22   45

5 Imagining the Land: A Duel of Descriptions in Numbers 13–14   59

6 Imagining the Temple in 2 Samuel 7:1–17   75

7 Performative Prayers of a Prophet: (Jon. 2:1–10 [2–11]; 4:2–3)   87

8 How to Do Things with Worlds   105

Bibliography   109

Index   115

About the Athor   119

Chapter 1

Speech Act Theory and Biblical Narrative

In literary studies, it is common to point out that villains do not typically see themselves as the antagonist of the story.[1] They view their (narrative) world in ways that differ from the other characters, especially the hero of the story. Other characters and even audiences may be drawn in by a villain's perspective for a variety of reasons, including a recognition of aspects that fit with their own experiences or worldviews.

Of course, villains are not the only characters in a story who may hold a subjective view of the world; every character can possess a unique perspective. One of the best modern examples of a storyteller utilizing this feature as a literary device is the comic strip *Calvin and Hobbes*. Created by Bill Watterson, *Calvin and Hobbes* follows the adventures of a boy named Calvin and a stuffed tiger named Hobbes. Whereas the other characters (e.g., Calvin's parents, teacher, classmates, and babysitter) see Hobbes as a stuffed animal, Calvin sees him as a real tiger and his best friend. Watterson describes the dynamic between Calvin and Hobbes as follows:

> Calvin sees Hobbes one way, and everyone else sees Hobbes another way. I show two versions of reality, and each makes complete sense to the participant who sees it. I think that's how life works. None of us sees the world in exactly the same way, and I just draw that literally in the strip. Hobbes is more about the subjective nature of reality than about dolls coming to life.[2]

Watterson uses his comic strip to explore many philosophical and theological topics in ways that entertain and captivate his readers as they engage with the characters.

I propose that viewing speeches within biblical narratives as speech acts reveals that these utterances can function in a manner that is similar to

1

Watterson's masterful use of pictures, both in presenting different viewpoints of the characters and in engaging the audience with these perspectives. In this book, I will utilize speech act theory (SAT) to analyze several biblical narratives in which characters use their words to portray their world (or aspects of their world) in different ways, often in an attempt to influence the actions of other characters. In addition, I will explore the ways in which the narrative worlds as they are presented by the storyteller may constitute an attempt to impact the audience. My methodology consists of two main components: (1) a narrative application of key aspects of SAT and (2) a distinction between two levels of narrative analysis: the story level and the storyteller level.

SPEECH ACT THEORY: RELEVANT COMPONENTS

A philosophy of language, SAT seeks to understand not only the meaning of words but also their performative power. As introduced by J.L. Austin in a series of lectures that were later compiled in a book entitled *How to Do Things with Words*, the guiding question of SAT is, "What does this utterance do?"[3] Austin argued that some utterances do more than merely convey ideas or describe the world, but can impact the world.[4] Austin opened the door to many others who have explored the performative nature of speech.[5]

Shifting the focus away from meaning (alone) to meaning that serves a purpose has made SAT a natural tool for practical theologians and biblical scholars who seek to understand the communicative functions of theological and biblical utterances. The question of "What does this utterance do?" can be applied to religious language ("What does this theological utterance do?") as well as to biblical texts ("What does this passage of Scripture do?") and biblical stories ("What does this story do?").[6] The theory has been utilized for approaching biblical hermeneutics as a whole, as well as a tool for analyzing specific biblical texts.[7] The present study examines ways in which the speech acts within biblical narratives create worlds from words; this is true for not only the narrative worlds that are created by the storytellers but also the various and often competing worlds that are displayed by the characters within the narrative world.

One of the challenges of using SAT in literary studies involves the high volume of technical terminology that appears in the many attempts to identify and categorize how speaking impacts the world.[8] It is easy to get lost in a discussion of the theory itself, and my aim here is to only share those aspects of SAT that are immediately helpful for this study. Specifically, I will focus on three aspects of SAT: (1) the distinction between illocutionary acts and perlocutionary acts, (2) a differentiation between five main illocutionary acts, and (3) a recognition of the impact that two particular variables have on the success of illocutionary acts, the sincerity condition and the direction of fit between words and the world.

The first feature of SAT that impacts this study involves distinguishing between two main categories of speech acts: illocutionary acts and perlocutionary acts. An illocutionary act can be defined as doing something *in* speaking, and a perlocutionary act involves achieving something *by* speaking. The success of an illocutionary act depends on the speaker who is acting in the context of the speech situation, whereas the success of a perlocutionary act also includes the response of the hearer.[9] For example, God's initial speech in Genesis 4 involves the performance of an illocutionary act of directing Cain to act rightly, be accepted, and resist sin in his situation (for more on this exchange, see chapter 2). While God successfully performs these illocutionary acts in speaking to Cain, the perlocutionary act of convincing Cain to act accordingly fails.

A second feature of SAT that is integral to this study is the taxonomy of illocutionary acts presented by John Searle, who suggests that every utterance constitutes at least one of five types of action.[10] Assertives are used to describe the world, while declaratives have the power to change the world. Directives prompt hearers to perform an action, and commissives commit the speaker to perform an action. Expressives display a speaker's emotional response to the world. These illocutionary acts may be illustrated by different uses of the word "strike" in the game of baseball.[11] While a single utterance can perform more than one illocutionary act, one of these five is usually the primary act (see table 1.1).

This leads into a third feature of SAT that is pertinent for this study, a recognition of certain variables as vital components of illocutionary acts. Speech

Table 1.1

Illocutionary Act	Speaker	Hearer	Speech	Performative Function
Directive	Manager	Pitcher	[Throw a] "Strike."	to direct someone
Commissive	Pitcher	Manager	[I will throw a] "Strike."	to commit oneself
Declarative	Umpire	Everyone watching	[I deem this a] "Strike!"	to affect and describe the world
Assertive	Announcer	Audience	[That was a] "Strike!"	to describe the world
Expressive	Player/Fan	Themselves and/or each other	"Strike!?"	to express feelings

act theorists have meticulously identified numerous variables that must be present in order for illocutionary acts to be successfully performed. For example, in order to successfully deem a pitch in a baseball game a "strike," one must be the umpire who is situated behind home plate. While Searle identifies many variables that may impact the success of an illocutionary act, he identifies two as most important to consider: the sincerity condition and the direction of fit between words and world (see table 1.2).[12]

The sincerity condition involves specific psychological states that must be expressed in order for the utterance to be successfully performed. Searle notes that actual sincerity is not required, but only the expression of sincerity; he points out that "insincere promises are promises nonetheless."[13] This recognition of the sincerity condition fits not only utterances in the real world but narrative worlds as well. For example, to defend their disobedience of Pharaoh's royal order to kill all the male Hebrew babies, Shiphrah and Puah claim that they are unable to serve as midwives due to an alleged difference between Hebrew women and Egyptian women (Exod. 1:15–19). In order to successfully perform this assertive, these midwives need only to appear to believe this assertive.[14]

The direction of fit involves the attempt to either match one's words to the world, or to affect the world with one's words. Early articulations of SAT focused on ways in which a speaker's words either match the world or impact the world, with declaratives having the performative power to do both and expressives lacking any such power. For example, in order to determine the success of an assertive that claims it to be raining outside, one would simply need to look outside. When applying SAT to a narrative, a character's speech act would be similarly weighed in how it fits with the narrative world.[15] Recent applications of SAT to narrative have included a "world-from-words"

Table 1.2

Illocutionary Act	Sincerity Condition	Explanation of Direction of Fit	Direction of Fit
Directive	Want	Words affect the world	World-to-words
Commissive	Intend	Words affect the world	World-to-words
Declarative	∅	Words affect the world and fit with the world	World-to-words & words-to-world
Assertive	Belief	Words fit with the world	Words-to-world
Expressive	= (Content is expressed)	Words need only fit with one's feelings about the world	None

direction of fit, recognizing that a storyteller's words have the power to create the narrative world.[16] At the same time, such a direction of fit might also exist within the narrative world itself. For example, the assertive that the midwives perform to Pharaoh regarding the state of how Hebrew women give birth does not need to fit with their narrative world, but only to the world as it exists in Pharaoh's imagination (see chapter 4).

STORY LEVEL AND STORYTELLER LEVEL

In discussing some of the challenges to the application of SAT to biblical interpretation, Briggs notes that the theory can be applied to more than one area of investigation:

> Speech acts can be considered in two fundamentally different spheres. Firstly, speech acts can be seen within the world of the text, from one character to another within a biblical narrative, for instance. Secondly, and in a completely different manner, there are the speech acts of the author or narrator, which address the reader of the text.[17]

These two distinct spheres need not be viewed as a hindrance to applying SAT to biblical texts, but can actually be a helpful way to organize the discussion and lead to levels of analysis that I call the story level and the storyteller level.

The distinction between the story level and storyteller level fits with similar approaches in narrative studies. In particular, it is customary for narrative critics to distinguish between the story level and the discourse level.[18] The story level involves the content, including the narrative's setting, events, dialogues, and plot. The discourse level looks for possible messages that the implied author may be trying to communicate to the implied audience based on how the story is told.[19] Pointing out that this kind of twofold distinction has been recognized since Aristotle's *Poetics*, Chapman says, "In simple terms, the story is the *what* in a narrative that is depicted, discourse is the *how*."[20] The present study will view the story level in a way that is consistent with how it is typically understood in literary studies, although the focus will specifically involve the function of the speech acts of the characters. The storyteller level will similarly incorporate the traditional understanding of discourse level but will also approach this topic from the perspective of SAT. As Goldingay points out, "Stories are designed to work, to do something. They are 'speech acts,' not just statements with propositional content but utterances with 'illocutionary force,' intended to effect something."[21] While the storyteller level includes the traditional understanding of the discourse level, it can broaden the focus to include aspects of interpretations that may be more closely associated with reader-response criticism. In other words, the storyteller level not only seeks conversations involving the (potential) intentions of an implied author but also invites responses to the story from real audiences that relate to the story in ways that may or may not fit with the storyteller's intentions.[22]

This study will illuminate the importance of the imagination for the successful performance of speech acts on both the story and storyteller levels. Within the discipline of biblical studies, no voice has been more influential on this topic than Walter Brueggemann. In the preface to the second edition of his groundbreaking book *The Prophetic Imagination*, Brueggemann claims that biblical texts "are acts of imagination that offer and purpose 'alternative worlds' that exist because of and in the act of utterance."[23] The recognition of the importance of imagination for literary analysis constitutes an important element of Brueggemann's methodology in much of his work.[24] One contribution I will make in this book is to demonstrate how the world-projecting power of speech is not only present among storytellers but functions on the story level through the speech acts of characters. Like storytellers, characters can perform speech acts that operate with a world-from-words direction of fit that matches the ways in which they imagine their narrative world.

SELECTED STORIES FOR THIS STUDY

While a SAT-infused literary approach can fit with any narrative study, the best results will likely be found in investigating stories that contain characters who describe their world in different ways and especially those that include exchanges where these views clash in some way.

Chapter 2 explores the story of Cain in Genesis 4 by identifying two diametrically opposed ways of viewing the world. Eve and Yhwh offer one view, as they imagine a world that resists human violence and celebrates God's relationship with humanity. This clashes with the views exhibited by Cain and Lamech, who operate in a violent world for their own selfish gains. While Cain and Lamech's imaginations (may) prevail on the story level, the storyteller critiques them as the audience is invited to celebrate and adopt the perspectives of Eve and Yhwh.

Chapter 3 investigates the role that asking questions might play in the success of certain intercessory prayers (Gen. 18:16–33; Exod. 32:7–14; and Amos 7:1–6). In these passages, Abraham, Moses, and Amos all use questions within their prayers that direct Yhwh's attention away from negative aspects of the situation and invite God to imagine the world in ways that may lead to a favorable response. In this way, the questions function as directives within the overall directive of the intercessory prayer. On the storyteller level, audiences are invited to consider the perlocutionary power of imagining the world in such a way.

Chapter 4 explores the role of Pharaoh's imagination in his efforts to reduce the strength and number of the Israelites in Exodus 1:8–22. After his first attempt fails, the midwives, Shiphrah and Puah, defend their disobedience to the king by appealing to an aspect of the toxic imaginary world that Pharaoh had previously cast. On the storyteller level, the midwives provide a practical example of putting the fear of God into action. This narrative also participates in numerous thematic and intertextual conversations that involve resisting oppressive imaginations.

Chapter 5 examines a crucial moment when the Israelite community must decide whether or not they will trust Yhwh and enter the land that God had promised to give them (Num. 13–14). After Moses sends spies into the land, they return to offer competing descriptions of the land; the adoption of one over the other will directly impact the community's decision. After the community chooses the worldview that constitutes a rejection of their God, Moses intercedes for them by offering Yhwh assertives that operate in a similar fashion to the prayers that were explored in chapter 3. On the storyteller level, this narrative provides a powerful portrayal of a prevalent depiction of Yhwh as someone who can forgive as well as bring punishment.

In chapter 6, the origin story of the conception of Solomon's temple and of Yhwh's covenant with David (2 Sam. 7:1–17) provides two different ways of imagining Yhwh's place and role among God's people. Assuming that God operates in ways that are similar to his own royal authority, King David proposes to build a house (temple) for God. Yhwh questions this plan and offers a different way of imagining how God might interact with the people in general and with David in particular. On the storyteller level, this narrative offers key insights that contribute to intertextual conversations regarding both the temple and God's covenant with David.

Chapter 7 will investigate the function(s) of Jonah's two prayers in the book of Jonah (Jon. 2:1–9 [2–10]; 4:2–3). Both prayers cast worlds that portray Jonah and Yhwh in particular ways. On the story level, Jonah performs his first prayer from the belly of a great fish and uses this prayer to portray himself as someone whom Yhwh might be expected to rescue. Jonah's second prayer provides his reasoning for initially disobeying Yhwh's directive to go to Nineveh. Both prayers highlight Yhwh's commitment (חֶסֶד), with the first prayer celebrating God's commitment to God's people (especially Jonah) and the second prayer bemoaning the extension of God's commitment outside such a community. On the storyteller level, audiences are invited to consider how Yhwh might relate to them and to others in ways that fit with God's amazing commitment.

Chapter 8 will offer a summary of the ways in which narrative worlds might be used to accomplish different goals. It will also suggest ways in which these worlds might impact the world of the audience.

NOTES

1. Portions of this chapter, especially the section regarding SAT, draw upon Steven T. Mann, "Let There Be Cain: A Clash of Imaginations in Genesis 4," *Journal for the Study of the Old Testament* 46 (2021): 79–95 (79–82). Used by permission.

2. Bill Watterson, *The Calvin and Hobbes Tenth Anniversary Book* (Kansas City: Andrews and McMeel, 1995), 22.

3. John L. Austin, *How to Do Things With Words*, eds. J. O. Urmson and Marina Sbisà (Cambridge, MA: Harvard University Press, 1975); John L. Austin, "Performative Utterances," in *Philosophical Papers*, eds. J. O. Urmson and G. J. Warnock (Oxford: Clarendon Press, 1970) 233–41. Repr. in *Philosophy of Language: The Big Questions*, ed. Andrea Nye (Malden, MA: Blackwell Publishers, 1998), 126–31.

4. One of Austin's examples is that by saying "I do" in the context of a wedding ceremony, one does more than describe the act of entering into a marriage. Similarly, making a bet with someone constitutes, rather than describes, a contract of sorts.

5. For a helpful overview of SAT, see Richard Briggs, "The Uses of Speech-Act Theory in Biblical Interpretation," *Currents in Research* 9 (2001): 229–76.

6. For an early example of exploring the performative nature of religious language, see Donald Evans, *The Logic of Self-Involvement: A Philosophical Study of Everyday Language with Special Reference to the Christian Use of Language about God as Creator* (London: SCM Press, 1963). Attempts to view biblical stories as speech acts include Roger Lundin, Anthony Thiselton, and Clarence Walhout, *The Responsibility of Hermeneutics* (Grand Rapids: Eerdmans, 1985); Nicholas Wolterstorff, "Living within a Text," in *Faith and Narrative*, ed. Keith E. Yandell (Oxford: Oxford University Press, 2001), 202–13.

7. For a recent articulation of SAT contributing to biblical interpretation as a whole, see Jeannine K. Brown, *Scripture as Communication: Introducing Biblical Hermeneutics* (Grand Rapids: Baker Academic, 2021), 21–24. For examples of SAT being used as a tool for interpreting specific portions of Scripture, see, e.g., Kristofer Holroyd, *A S(Word) against Babylon. An Examination of the Multiple Speech Act Layers within Jeremiah 50–51* (Winona Lake: Eisenbrauns, 2017); Steven T. Mann, *Run, David, Run! An Investigation of the Theological Speech Acts of David's Departure and Return (2 Samuel 14–20)* (Winona Lake: Eisenbrauns, 2013).

8. Briggs, "The Uses of Speech-Act Theory," 230. Douglas Mangum and Wendy Widder, "Speech Act Theory," *The Lexham Bible Dictionary* (Bellingham, WA: Lexham Press, 2016).

9. The speech situation consists of the many conditions within which a speech act is uttered, including (but not limited to) the identity of the speaker and the hearer, the relationship between them, and the larger context of the conversation. For the role of conversation in speech acts, see H. P. Grice, "Meaning,"

in *Philosophy of Language: The Big Questions*, ed. Andrea Nye (Malden, MA: Blackwell, 1998), 118–25; H. P. Grice, "Logic and Conversation," in *Syntax and Semantics,* vol. 3: *Speech Acts*, eds. P. Cole and J. Morgan (New York: Academic Press, 1975), 41–58.

10. John Searle, *Speech Acts*: *An Essay in the Philosophy of Language* (London: Cambridge University Press, 1969); John Searle, *Expression and Meaning*: *Studies in the Theory of Speech Acts* (New York: Cambridge University Press, 1979), viii.

11. Steven T. Mann, "Performative Prayers of a Prophet: Investigating the Prayers of Jonah as Speech Acts," *Catholic Biblical Quarterly* 79 (2017): 20–40 (21–23).

12. Searle, *Expression and Meaning*, 1–3.

13. Searle, *Expression and Meaning*, 62.

14. See chapter 4 for a discussion of this exchange between Pharaoh and the midwives.

15. For a further discussion on applying SAT to narratives, see Mann, *Run, David, Run*, 41–45.

16. For a further discussion of a "world-from-words" direction of fit, see Mann, *Run, David, Run*, 45–49.

17. Briggs, "The Uses of Speech-Act Theory," 230.

18. E.g., see Seymour Chatman, *Story and Discourse: Narrative Structure in Fiction and Film* (Ithaca: Cornell University, 1978). For an application of this distinction in biblical studies, see Mark Allan Powell, *What Is Narrative Criticism?* (Minneapolis: Fortress Press, 1990), 23–34.

19. The concepts of implied authors and implied audiences are common in narrative studies. For an overview of the distinction between real and implied authors and audiences, as well as the distinction between the narrator and the implied author, see Chapman, *Story and Discourse,* 147–58; Powell, *What Is Narrative Criticism,* 23–27.

20. Chatman, *Story and Discourse*, 19. Chatman goes on to point out that "For Aristotle, the imitation of actions in the real world, *praxis,* was seen as forming an argument, *logos,* from which were selected (and possibly rearranged) the units that formed the plot, *mythos*" (Italics original).

21. John Goldingay, *Models for Interpretation of Scripture* (Toronto: Clements, 1995), 65.

22. This interpretive approach, especially as it pertains to stories found in Scripture, fits with Powell's point regarding the continuing impact of "classic" stories as "a work that continues to be meaningful in times and places that were not originally envisioned by the author." Mark Allan Powell, "Narrative Criticism," in *Hearing the New Testament: Strategies for Interpretation*, ed. Joel B. Green (Grand Rapids: Eerdmans, 2010), 240–58 (242).

23. Walter Brueggemann, *The Prophetic Imagination*, 2nd ed. (Minneapolis: Fortress Press, 2001), x.

24. For example, Brueggemann builds upon Sigmund Mowinckel's recognition of the "world-making" power of worship in his short yet insightful book, *Spirituality of the Psalms* (Minneapolis: Fortress Press, 2002). See also and especially Brueggemann's overview of selected "authoritative voices" for methodologies that explore the ways in which texts create worlds in Walter Brueggemann, *Divine Presence Amid Violence: Contextualizing the Book of Joshua* (Eugene, OR: Cascade Books, 2009), 5–6.

Chapter 2

A Clash of Imaginations in Genesis 4

A good story often has a great villain.[1] As the infamous murderer of Abel in Genesis 4, Cain is not only a memorable villain but also the main character. This is shown by the amount of space devoted to Cain in the passage and in the way in which every speech in the story involves Cain. Every speaker either offers words about Cain, words directed to Cain, or words uttered by Cain.

This chapter will focus on the Cain-oriented speech acts as follows: Eve's speech about Cain's birth (v. 1b), the two exchanges between Yhwh and Cain (vv. 6–7 & 9–15), Lamech's speech to his wives (vv. 23–24), and Eve's speech about Seth's birth (v. 25). On the story level, Eve and Yhwh imagine the world in ways that resist human sin and violence and that celebrate God's relationship with humanity. Cain and Lamech reject this notion and choose to focus only on themselves. On the storyteller level, the speech acts of Genesis 4 invite the audience to adopt and celebrate the imaginations of Eve and Yhwh and to reject the imaginations of Cain and Lamech.

EVE'S SPEECH ABOUT CAIN'S BIRTH (V. 1B)

Eve speaks after bearing Cain saying, "I have created a man with Yhwh" (קָנִיתִי אִישׁ אֶת־יהוה) (v. 1).[2] While the narrator does not explicitly say here that Eve is the person who names Cain, this might be inferred by the wordplay between his name (קַיִן) and her self-described action (קָנִיתִי). This assumption also holds merit in light of Eve's later act of naming Seth (see Gen. 4:25), which is followed by an assertive that utilizes a wordplay between the name (שֵׁת) and the accompanying explanation (utilizing שָׁת).[3]

11

Story Level

The act of naming Cain functions as a declarative, but Eve's speech act here occurs after that act as an assertive. Interpreters have noted the oddity of Eve's assertive in that it does not match a typical birth report saying.[4] Indeed, Eve's assertive is one that imagines her identity as a creator, emphasizing her role as Yhwh's partner (not Adam's partner) and creating a man (אִישׁ), rather than giving birth to a baby.[5]

Some interpreters respond favorably to Eve's imagination, while others resist it. Schneider notes that Eve's statement emphasizes her participation with God in the creative act. She says,

> Eve's statement highlights that she considers herself involved in the process of creation, working with the Deity. The creation verb Eve uses is one of the verbs used to refer to the Divine's role in creation (14:19, 22; Deut. 32:6), and of the Deity redeeming the people. (Exod. 15:16; Isa. 11:11)[6]

Other interpreters balk at elevating Eve to God's level, translating קנה as "acquire" and qualifying Eve's accomplishment as done "with the help of" Yhwh.[7] Nevertheless, a translation that Eve has "created a man" fits with the stem, especially in light of its use in Ugaritic texts such as Atiratu's epithet "Creatress of the gods" (*qnyt. 'ilym*).[8] Galambush calls the addition of "with the help of [Yhwh]" conjectural and suggests that Eve says, "I produced a man, like Yhwh did!"[9] Galambush goes on to suggest that "Eve seems surprised and delighted at her accomplishment."[10] An opposite reaction is offered by Rosenberg. After translating Eve's statement as "I have created a man as Yahweh has," he goes on to say, "I read Eve's assertion as an ironic, narcissistic mistake on her part."[11] The negative reaction by some (often male) interpreters to Eve's assertive further demonstrates how her identity and role in the world, as portrayed by her assertive, challenges their own imaginations.

Storyteller Level

On the storyteller level, Eve's assertive utilizes an imagination that counters several aspects of the depiction of Eve in the passage that precedes this story in Genesis. The consequences of human disobedience as described in Genesis 3 (commonly called "the Fall") depict the woman bearing children in pain/toil (עצב) and enduring the man's dominion over her.[12] The only time that Yhwh speaks to Eve in Genesis 3 is when God describes her future struggles. In the context of the book of Genesis, Eve's assertive counters these three earlier portrayals as follows: (1) it resists male authority over women (patriarchy),

(2) it provides an alternative depiction of childbearing, and (3) it demonstrates that Eve's relationship with Yhwh does not rely on her connection with a man. Eve's assertive at the opening of Genesis 4 invites readers to imagine the identity and authority of women in ways that counter the world that is on display in Genesis 3.

First, Eve's speech act resists male dominion. De Groot notes, "Given the patriarchal cast of the text, the naming of the children by the mother is surprising. It puts Eve in a parallel role to the man."[13] In addition to naming her son, the lack of Adam's name in Eve's assertive is particularly striking given its proximity to the man naming Eve in Genesis 3:20. Male interpreters sometimes point out that Eve could not have produced Cain by herself (a similar point can be made of the men who are said to become fathers without naming the mothers in the list of descendants of Adam in Gen. 5). Nevertheless, Eve's statement shows that she needs no man, and she resists the man's governance by naming her son and omitting reference to the man from this assertive.

Eve's assertive also casts a drastic contrast to the portrayal of childbearing in the passage that immediately precedes it. Whereas in Genesis 3 childbearing is described as a painful process, Eve casts it as an act of creation without mentioning any struggle. In claiming credit along with Yhwh, this speech testifies that Yhwh has not abandoned Eve to her fate. This fits with a greater theme in Genesis and throughout Scripture, which after speaking of consequences Yhwh still might act with grace.

Eve's speech also displays herself as in a relationship with God that is not defined by a connection with a husband.[14] As Schneider points out, "her comments upon the birth of her first and third sons address her relationship not with her husband but with the Deity (4:1, 25)."[15] Meyers suggests that Eve's utterance holds significance for viewing all women alongside God. She points out:

> [T]he word for "create" is the same as the word used in the Bible for the creative power of God (Gen 14:19, 22) and in extrabiblical texts for the creativity of Semitic mother goddesses. Women in the Bible are said to "bear children," not "create a man"; and creating a man "with" God puts female creative power alongside that of God.[16]

Previously in Genesis, Yhwh speaks to the man several times (Gen. 2:26; 3:9–12, 17–19) and to the woman only in regard to the consequences of her actions (Gen. 3:13, 16). Here Eve's relationship with God is shown to have continued and has grown into one that consists of partners.

THE FIRST EXCHANGE BETWEEN
YHWH AND CAIN (VV. 6–7)

The narrator sets up the situation in which the exchange between Cain and
Yhwh will take place by describing Yhwh's response to offerings made to
God by both Abel and Cain. After sharing the occupation of each individual
(v. 2b), the narrator gives a description of their offerings (vv. 3–4a) that
are made in accordance with their respective occupations. A description of
Yhwh's response to each man and his offering follows (vv. 4b–5a), and then
the narrator shares Cain's negative reaction (v. 5b). Interpreters have offered
potential reasons for why Abel's offering is accepted and Cain's is not, with
many suggesting that Abel's act of bringing the firstfruits indicates that Cain
alternately did not bring a suitable sacrifice. While such an interpretation is
possible on the storyteller level, on the story level neither Abel nor Cain is
instructed on how to bring an offering, and neither man receives an explanation of Yhwh's acceptance (or lack thereof) of his offering.[17] Cain's reaction
to Yhwh's response sets up Yhwh's interaction with Cain.

Story Level

On the story level, Yhwh performs a series of speech acts that attempt to shift
Cain's focus from the past to the present, with the purpose of persuading him
to resist sin's influence in the immediate future. The speech fits into a poetic
structure with seven lines (see table 2.1).

Yhwh first asks three questions that function as directives with indirect
assertives. That is, Yhwh directs Cain to reflect on his present situation and
then to imagine a situation where he is accepted. Yhwh then utters three
assertives that imagine the world of Cain not acting in a way that will lead to
his acceptance, and then issues one main directive for how Cain is to act in
such a situation.

Yhwh's questions serve as directives for Cain to move forward from his
disappointment and act appropriately in the present and future. The first two
questions prompt Cain to consider the reason for his mood. They also operate

Table 2.1

v. 6ba	לָמָּה חָרָה לָךְ	Why are you angry?	Directive (+ Assertive)
v. 6bb	וְלָמָּה נָפְלוּ פָנֶיךָ	And why has your face fallen?	Directive (+ Assertive)
v. 7aa	הֲלוֹא אִם־תֵּיטִיב שְׂאֵת	If you do well, will you not be accepted?	Directive (+ Assertive)
v. 7ab	וְאִם לֹא תֵיטִיב	And if you do not do well,	Assertive
v. 7ac	לַפֶּתַח חַטָּאת רֹבֵץ	At the door sin is lurking;	Assertive
v. 7ba	וְאֵלֶיךָ תְּשׁוּקָתוֹ	For you is its desire	Assertive
v. 7bb	וְאַתָּה תִּמְשָׁל־בּוֹ	And you must master it.	Directive

Table 2.2

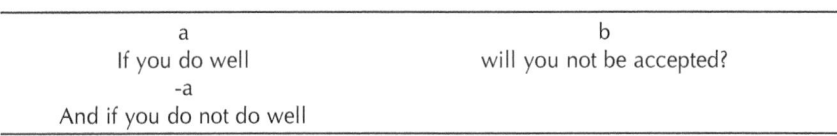

a	b
If you do well	will you not be accepted?
-a	
And if you do not do well	

as assertives that acknowledge Cain's troubled emotional state. If Yhwh had stopped speaking after asking the first two questions, Yhwh's utterance might be understood as a perlocutionary act to help Cain process why neither he nor his offering was accepted. But by asking a third question, Yhwh reveals that the purpose is to help Cain move forward. The assertive attached to the third question involves Cain doing well and being accepted, inviting Cain to imagine being accepted by God.

Yhwh's assertives then describe the world in which Cain does not do well, a world in which sin is lurking at the door and desiring Cain.[18] This is the world that matches Cain's current imagination. The antithetical parallelism includes a conspicuous omission that fits within Yhwh's aforementioned purpose of helping Cain to move forward from his current state. The parallelism of the first assertive begins in a straightforward relationship to the question that precedes it: (see table 2.2).

The corresponding section might be expected to follow the pattern and say something like "you will not be accepted (-b)." Instead, Yhwh speaks of sin lurking and desiring Cain. In this way, Yhwh attempts to redirect Cain's focus from having not been accepted and enables Cain to see that the reality of his present situation requires him to act appropriately. Yhwh completes the speech with the straightforward directive for Cain to master sin.

Cain's response shows that Yhwh's perlocutionary act has failed on the story level. Cain does not directly respond to Yhwh, but turns instead to speak to Abel as a sort of non-speech act in his interaction with Yhwh. The utterance itself, a directive and commissive for the brothers to go out to the field (v. 8ab), is famously missing in the MT.[19] Nevertheless, the speech formula alone of "Cain said to his brother Abel" (v. 8aa) suggests that Cain is choosing to ignore Yhwh and, by extension, submit to sin's dominion.

Storyteller Level

On the storyteller level, interpreters have noticed the way in which Yhwh's first speech introduces the theme of sin. The first appearance of this word in Scripture, sin in this context consists of "one human being's violence to another."[20] Cotter suggests that this "implies that all sin is somehow fratricide."[21] In the grand narrative that runs throughout the Bible, readers can see this as the beginning of God's struggle against sin's hold on humanity. While there are instances elsewhere in Scripture where God will stop someone from sinning (e.g., Gen. 20:6; 1 Sam. 25:26), this is the first of many instances where God attempts to persuade people to resist sin's influence.

THE RESULTING EXCHANGES BETWEEN
YHWH AND CAIN (VV. 9–15)

After a brief report of the murder of Abel (v. 8b), the scene turns back to Yhwh and Cain. The pace of the story then slows down to reveal a conversation containing two exchanges (v. 9 and vv. 10–15), both of which are initiated by questions from Yhwh (see tables 2.3 and 2.4).

Story Level

Yhwh's questions function as directives for Cain to think about his brother Abel (v. 9) and then to face the consequences of his crime against his brother (v. 10).

Table 2.3

v. 9ab	אֵי הֶבֶל אָחִיךָ	Where is Abel, your brother?	Directive
v. 9bb	לֹא יָדַעְתִּי הֲשֹׁמֵר אָחִי אָנֹכִי	I do not know. Am I my brother's keeper?	Assertive, Directive
v. 10ab	מֶה עָשִׂיתָ	What have you done?	Directive/ Expressive
v. 10b	קוֹל דְּמֵי אָחִיךָ צֹעֲקִים אֵלַי מִן־הָאֲדָמָה׃	The voice of your brother's blood is crying out to me from the ground!	Assertive
v. 11	וְעַתָּה אָרוּר אָתָּה מִן־הָאֲדָמָה אֲשֶׁר פָּצְתָה אֶת־פִּיהָ לָקַחַת אֶת־דְּמֵי אָחִיךָ מִיָּדֶךָ׃	And now you are cursed from the ground, which opened its mouth to receive the blood of your brother from your hand.	Declarative
v. 12	כִּי תַעֲבֹד אֶת־הָאֲדָמָה לֹא־תֹסֵף תֵּת־כֹּחָהּ לָךְ נָע וָנָד תִּהְיֶה בָאָרֶץ׃	When you serve the ground, it will no longer give to you its strength; a fugitive and a wanderer you will be in the land.	Assertives

Yhwh's question of "Where is Abel, your brother?" is a directive that requests information from Cain regarding the location of Abel. The designation of Abel as "your brother" continues to highlight the connection between Cain and Abel that is also emphasized on the storyteller level, and so Yhwh's utterance is also a directive for Cain to reflect on his responsibility to his brother.[22] As a perlocutionary act, Yhwh may be attempting to persuade Cain to admit to his crime and repent.[23]

Cain's response demonstrates that Yhwh's illocutionary acts, but not the perlocutionary act, have been marginally successful. The assertive "I do not know" responds to Yhwh's illocutionary act of requesting information about Abel's whereabouts, albeit insincerely. As a rhetorical question, the ensuing directive of "Am I my brother's keeper?" also functions as an assertive that dismisses any responsibility for Cain to know of his brother's whereabouts. Cain has reflected upon his responsibility to his brother, but with negative results. Riemann points out that the use of "keeper" with "my brother" shows a striking disdain for Abel, since it would be animals, not humans, who need keepers.[24] In this way Cain not only denies responsibility for Abel, but dehumanizes his brother.

Yhwh responds to Cain with a directive in the form of the question, "What have you done?!" In this way, Yhwh seeks to make Cain confront his deed.[25] On the other hand, Sarna points out that this is "not a question, but a cry of horror,"[26] which would also make it an expressive. The ensuing assertive supports both of these functions of Yhwh's opening speech act by describing the world as it exists from Yhwh's perspective, that Abel's blood has been crying out to God from the ground. Many translations recognize that this assertive is also functioning as a directive and thus add the command, "Listen!" Indeed, Yhwh is attempting to prompt Cain to view the world from a divine perspective.

The next portion of Yhwh's speech consists of a curse, a powerful declarative. As both a pronouncement and enactment of Cain's sentence, Yhwh's declarative changes Cain's relationship to the ground and with it his own identity. The way in which Cain is "cursed from the ground" has yielded much scholarly discussion regarding the nature and effects of the curse. Cassuto offers a helpful explanation that is based on the chiastic ordering of "your brother's blood" (A, A') and "from the ground" (B, B') in verses 10-11 (A, B, B', A'):

> The parallelism . . . shows that the principle of measure for measure is applied here, and that the expression *from the ground* in [verse 11] must be understood in the very same sense in which it is used in the previous verse. Hence it is not to be interpreted, with some commentators, as meaning *more than the ground* . . . or *far from the [cultivated] ground* . . .; nor is it to be deleted as a duplication taken over from v. 10 . . . The correct explanation is: your curse shall come

upon you from the ground, just as the cry of your brother's blood came to me from the ground (Ibn Ezra: "through the ground").[27]

The practical implications of Cain's curse coming from the ground are then described by Yhwh's assertives. The ground will now fail to produce in response to Cain's efforts, and Cain will (thus) have a new identity as a fugitive and a wanderer.

The conversation continues as Cain laments his punishment and Yhwh responds with grace (see table 2.4). Cain begins his protest with an expressive by which he shares his feeling that his sin and punishment are greater than he can bear.[28] As an expressive, the sentiment need not be true to the world but only to Cain's feelings and fit with Cain's imagination. Cain then performs a series of assertives that describe the situation, from his perspective, that has resulted from Yhwh's declarative. Cain summarizes the impact of the curse, accusing Yhwh of driving him away from the face of the ground and from Yhwh's face. He then repeats Yhwh's assertive in describing his identity as a fugitive and a wanderer. However, Cain then adds an assertive of his own describing the violent reaction that people will have when they encounter him. It is not clear why Cain imagines that his life will be at risk. Perhaps he fears retribution by a kinsman redeemer (hence his identity as fugitive),[29] or perhaps Cain views such a threat to be simply a part of what it means to be a wanderer.

Yhwh responds to Cain by issuing a declarative that counters the assertive that Cain had added to the description of his situation. The MT begins Yhwh's utterance with "therefore," while the LXX, Peshitta, and Vulgate start with "Not so." While both words emphasize that Yhwh's utterance is

Table 2.4

v. 13b	גָּדוֹל עֲוֹנִי מִנְּשֹׂא:	My punishment is greater than I can lift!	Expressive
v. 14	הֵן גֵּרַשְׁתָּ אֹתִי הַיּוֹם מֵעַל פְּנֵי הָאֲדָמָה וּמִפָּנֶיךָ אֶסָּתֵר וְהָיִיתִי נָע וָנָד בָּאָרֶץ וְהָיָה כָל־מֹצְאִי יַהַרְגֵנִי:	Here, you have driven me today away from the face of the ground, and from your face I will be hidden. And I will be a fugitive and a wanderer in the land, and anyone who finds me will slay me.	Assertives
v. 15b	לָכֵן כָּל־הֹרֵג קַיִן שִׁבְעָתַיִם יֻקָּם	Therefore [/Not so] anyone who slays Cain will experience a sevenfold vengeance.	Declarative [/Assertive]

attached to Cain's speech, the word "therefore" emphasizes the declarative illocutionary force. Yhwh does not merely counter Cain's assertive that he will be killed with another assertive to the contrary. Neither does Yhwh offer a commissive promising to personally protect Cain, as Yhwh will later offer Abraham (see Gen. 12:3). Rather, with this declarative Yhwh addresses the additional aspect of the world as described by Cain by imposing a punishment on anyone who will act as Cain expects.[30] The declarative force of the utterance is also shown by Yhwh's use of the third person instead of the second person for this utterance. Many interpreters have focused on the protective mark that Yhwh places on Cain immediately after delivering this declarative.[31] However, the mark alone does not have the power; the performative word of Yhwh has the power, with the mark either signifying or working alongside the performative word.[32]

Cain leaves Yhwh's presence and settles in the land of Nod, or "Wandering," east of Eden. While it may seem odd that after being turned into a wanderer Cain settles, the name of the location may provide an answer for how he can both settle and be a wanderer. The ensuing part of Cain's story demonstrates that Yhwh's declarative has been a successful perlocutionary act. Rather than meeting people who will kill him, Cain meets a wife, has a son, and builds a city.

Storyteller Level

Cain's response to Yhwh is one of the most powerful speech acts in Scripture, as both the rest of Scripture and countless listening audiences have been drawn in by Cain's question, "Am I my brother's keeper?" While a rhetorical question on the story level, on the storyteller level audiences have followed Cain's directive to reflect not only on Cain's situation but on humanity as a whole. Boesak points out that the story of Cain and Abel "is a very human story that is still being enacted today" and goes on to say:

> What was Cain's responsibility with respect to his brother Abel? He did not have the responsibility to be Abel's keeper. Neither was his responsibility to be Abel's ruler. Nor was he Abel's guardian. His responsibility, rather, was to be Abel's brother. This responsibility involves being human in community with one another in God's world.[33]

Sarna also connects Cain with humanity, noting that "The sevenfold stress in this chapter on the obvious fraternal relationship of Cain and Abel emphatically teaches that [humanity] is indeed [their] brother's keeper and that all homicide is fratricide."[34]

Cain's question also introduces a theme that resonates throughout Scripture, which gives an affirmative answer. For example, in the Torah, ancient Israel is instructed to provide an heir for a deceased brother (Deut. 25:5–6). If they see an ox belonging to their neighbor wandering away, they must bring it back (Deut. 22:1–4). Similarly, if they see the ox of their enemy going astray or struggling, they are to relieve it from the burden (Exod. 23:4–5). When they reap a harvest, Israel is taught to leave a portion of it for the poor to glean (Lev. 19:9–10, 23.22). They are to lend money to the poor without interest (Exod. 22:25–27), and to provide for the orphan, widow, and immigrant (e.g., Deut. 10:18–19, 24:17–22). They are not to hate in their heart anyone of their kin, and they are to love their neighbor as themselves (Lev. 19:17–18).

The audience may go on to note the irony that the only person who has acted in violence is the one who now fears he will be a victim. Interpreters have wondered why Yhwh does not kill Cain for the crime of murder, in light of later teachings in the Torah that indicate such a sentence. However, Yhwh's act of grace here fits well with the opening chapters of Genesis, as this is the second time in Genesis where Yhwh has not punished humans with death for a transgression that is attached to the punishment of death (cf. Gen. 2:17 in light of Yhwh's reaction to Adam and Eve in Gen. 3).

The exchange between Yhwh and Cain invites the audience to imagine God as someone who seeks to encourage humanity to live in relationship with one another in ways that seek to protect the weaker parties. While Yhwh fails to change Cain's imagination regarding his role as Abel's brother, the story has had some success in encouraging the listening audience to see their fellow humans as family. While history (as well as modern events) reveals that humans often choose the violent ways of Cain, there remains the beckoning alternative imagination of God in which sin does not have the final word.

LAMECH'S SPEECH TO ADAH AND ZILLAH (VV. 23–24)

Story Level

The narrator sets up the next utterance in the passage, Lamech's poetic speech to his wives, with a birth report of Cain's son and his act of building a city named after his son. This is followed by a genealogy that extends from Enoch to Lamech and includes the names of Lamech's two wives, Adah and Zillah. The names of their respective offspring are offered (two sons of Adah and a son and a daughter for Zillah), along with a description of the male's descendants' occupations.[35]

While a story is embedded in Lamech's speech, this poetic utterance stands alone without an accompanying narrative. His speech consists of parallel directives, parallel assertives, and parallel declaratives (see table 2.5).

Table 2.5

v. 23ab	עֲדָה וְצִלָּה שְׁמַעַן קוֹלִי	Adah and Zillah, hear my voice;	Directive
v. 23ac	נְשֵׁי לֶמֶךְ הַאְזֵנָּה אִמְרָתִי	Women of Lamech, listen to what I say:	Directive
v. 23ba	כִּי אִישׁ הָרַגְתִּי לְפִצְעִי	For a man I have slain for wounding me,	Assertive
v. 23bb	וְיֶלֶד לְחַבֻּרָתִי:	a young man for striking me.	Assertive
v. 24a	כִּי שִׁבְעָתַיִם יֻקַּם־קָיִן	For Cain will be avenged sevenfold,	Declarative
v. 24b	וְלֶמֶךְ שִׁבְעִים וְשִׁבְעָה:	Surely Lamech seventy-sevenfold.	Declarative

The directives introduce Lamech's speech and direct his audience to listen. The assertives recount Lamech's act of killing a man and his reason for doing so. The two declaratives work together, with the second declarative expanding Yhwh's previous declarative to Cain so that it includes Lamech.

Interpreters have viewed Lamech's entire speech to be an act of boasting of his violence.[36] Lamech's description of the event portrays him escalating the violence done to him, responding to a wound and strike with murder. In his imagination, Lamech has acted rightly and wants his wives to know of his achievement. Schneider points out that it is not clear why Lamech addresses his wives "since there is little in his statement that concerns the women."[37] Niditch asks, "Does he want to impress them with his prowess? Does he wish to encourage them to compose a woman's victory song of their own for him (see Judg. 5; Exod. 15.20–21?)"[38] Meyers suggests an affirmative answer to the latter question, stating that "the prominent role of women as musicians includes the custom of women composing and performing victory psalms or songs (as by Miriam and Deborah) following an outstanding military victory."[39] If this is the case, then Lamech's poem is a (failed) perlocutionary act of eliciting such a song.

Lamech completes his poem with two lines that adopt and intensify Yhwh's protective declarative to Cain. Some interpreters have viewed this as a threat of future violence to potential adversaries, a commissive in which Lamech threatens to continue to proliferate violence. It is also possible to view these lines as assertives that look back and describe Lamech's aforementioned act. While these interpretations are possible, the reference to Cain makes it more likely that Lamech is building on Yhwh's declarative, first by referencing it (v. 24a) and then adding himself to the declarative and intensifying it (v. 24b). Like Cain, Lamech imagines that his violent actions will bring violent reactions, and Lamech seeks to protect himself by hijacking Yhwh's protective utterance for Cain.

The scene closes abruptly without any response by Adah and Zillah. There is no indication from the narrator that Lamech's perlocutionary act of protecting his own life has been successful, and the audience is left wondering what just happened.

Storyteller Level

On the storyteller level, Lamech's speech holds significance for understanding the practical nature of Cain's story. Structurally, the placement of
Lamech's story (Gen. 4:17–24) between two telling of Cain's crime against
Abel (Gen. 4:1–16; 25–26) creates a chiasm that invites the audience to discuss Lamech's story in light of that of Cain. Lamech is portrayed as someone
who believes that Cain's story holds relevance for his own life. In this way,
Lamech serves as an exemplar audience member, a link between the story and
storyteller levels of Cain's story. Unfortunately, Lamech has adopted Cain's
imagination instead of Yhwh's imagination.

    On the storyteller level, the descriptions of the women in Lamech's life
function as a foil to Lamech, a critique of his boasting. Meyers points out that
the names of the three women stand out as they are the only females included
in the genealogies of Genesis 1–10.[40] She notes that their descendants are
"founders of the civilized arts, which are thus presented as a fully human
product and not as a gift of the gods, as in many mythological beginnings
stories of other cultures."[41] Furthermore, their contribution "acknowledges
that human creativity is inextricably linked to female parentage."[42] Schneider
agrees, stating:

> The appearance of Adah and Zillah, the roles their children play, and the mean-
> ing of their names combine to highlight these women as factors in the develop-
> ment of society and, even with the first mothers, how important a role they play
> in civilization. This case too indicates that their role as mothers is at least as
> important as their role as wives.[43]

While Adah and Zillah do not speak on the story level, the names of these
women and the description of their contributions to society elevate the status
of these women. As a result, their silence after Lamech's poem may serve
as a rejection of his imagination. It is not surprising that interpreters usually
view Lamech negatively; the storyteller reserves all positive contributions to
his wives rather than to him.

    One aspect of Lamech's speech that deserves more attention is the manner
in which Lamech uses Yhwh's declarative for his own protection. Indeed,
through Lamech, the storyteller reveals the tendency of humans to select
among Yhwh's words only those that fit with their own purposes and protection, rather than seeking to follow Yhwh's will. The listening and self-
reflective audience might notice this passage's critique of humanity and dare
to consider ways in which they and/or their communities might exhibit Cain
and Lamech's violent and paranoid imaginations.

EVE'S SPEECH ON SETH'S BIRTH (V. 25)

Story Level

The passage concludes with one more brief utterance from Eve, delivered after a birth report. Here, the man Adam is named, whereas Eve is described as "his woman," thus reversing their respective introductions at the beginning of the pericope.

As with her earlier assertive regarding Cain's name, this assertive explains Eve's decision to name her child. Seth's name holds significance to the way in which God has "appointed" another child for Eve "instead of Abel, because Cain killed him" (v. 25). The meaning of Seth appears to be melancholy, although Sarna has noted that the meaning of the noun שֵׁת as "foundation" might include an element of hope.[44] Nevertheless, with this assertive Eve not only looks forward but also backward, connecting Seth's name to Cain's act of murdering Abel. Seth will serve as an enduring reminder of Cain's crime against Abel.

Storyteller Level

At this point, the audience might feel a bit like time travelers. They might wonder why the storyteller did not place this brief birth report immediately after Cain's final interaction with Yhwh. In addition to the effect of the chiastic structuring (see above), by placing this Cain-oriented speech act at the end of the passage, the storyteller ensures that Eve, not Lamech, has the final word. It also serves as a reminder not only of Cain's violence but as a tribute to the enduring memory of Cain's brother, Abel.[45] Furthermore, the reference to Seth's line redirects the audience away from Cain's line that ends in violence and allows the story to continue in a way that follows Eve's imagination, which leads to people invoking the name of Yhwh (v. 26).

The importance of Eve's voice is also suggested on the storyteller level by a striking feature of the introduction of Eve's assertive. The Hebrew for this speech strangely lacks a speech formula that introduces the woman's assertive. Instead, there is only the preposition כִּי ("for/because"). While the LXX and Targums add the formula "she said," here in the MT this speech blends the voice of the narrator and the woman: "And Adam again knew his woman, and she bore a son and she called his name Seth, for God has appointed for me another child instead of Abel, for Cain killed him." Here at the end of the story, the narrator looks out at the audience as a woman who can successfully utter this assertive without first introducing it in the mouth of the woman on the story level.

The blending of the voice of the woman and the narrator continues with the storyteller's final assertives of the birth of Seth's son Enosh and then of humanity beginning to invoke Yhwh's name. In the beginning of Genesis 4, it is Eve who speaks Yhwh's name and connects Cain to Yhwh; at the end of the story, the narrator's speech connects Yhwh to all humanity. Hence, the female storyteller invites the audience into a relationship with God that is similar to God's relationship with Cain. The audience must choose if they will respond positively to Yhwh's encouragement and direction, or if they will respond in ways similar to Cain and Lamech.

CONCLUSIONS

This chapter has demonstrated that the Cain-oriented speech acts in Genesis 4 function on both the story level and storyteller level by appealing to the imagination of both the characters and the audience. Furthermore, this investigation has identified a clash of imaginations on display in these speech acts, with Eve and Yhwh on one side and Cain and Lamech on the other.

On the story level, Eve pushes back against numerous patriarchal assumptions with her speeches. Not only does she resist male authority by naming Cain, but she celebrates her role in producing Cain as an event occurring within a partnership with Yhwh. Such a perspective of the world fits with the equality of all humanity that is on display in Genesis 1:26–27 and critiques the description of Eve's predicament in Genesis 3:16. Similarly, Yhwh's speeches to Cain push back against the assumption that sin must have dominion in the world. From Yhwh's perspective, sin can be overcome. The words of Eve and Yhwh thus create a world in which humans resist sin and violence and celebrate God's relationship with humanity. Cain and Lamech, however, reject such notions and choose to focus only on themselves. In failing to respond to Yhwh's guidance on mastering sin, Cain rejects Yhwh's imagination of how to act in the world and chooses violence and self-preservation. Cain's perspective is later shared, advanced, and celebrated by Lamech, who employs Yhwh's previous utterance for his own selfish and sadistic purposes.

On the storyteller level, the speech acts of Genesis 4 invite the audience to adopt and celebrate the imaginations of Eve and Yhwh, and to recognize and then rid themselves of the toxic imaginations of Cain and Lamech.

NOTES

1. A previous version of this chapter was published as Steven T. Mann, "Let There Be Cain: A Clash of Imaginations in Genesis 4," *Journal for the Study of the Old Testament* 46, no. 1 (2021): 79–95 (79–82). Used by permission.

2. Unless otherwise noted, translations of the MT as it appears in *The Hebrew Bible: Andersen-Forbes Analyzed Text* (Francis I. Andersen; A. Dean Forbes, 2008) are the author's own. A focus on this final form of the text is not intended to dismiss the many investigations regarding the complexities involving the origins, formation, and translations of this or any passage. For a discussion of recent European scholarship on the origins and formation of Genesis, see Thomas B. Dozeman, Konrad Schmid, and Baruch J. Schwartz, eds., *The Pentateuch: International Perspectives on Current Research* (Tubingen: Mohr Siebeck, 2011). For a discussion of ancient translations, traditions, and interpretations of the story of Cain and Abel in Genesis 4, especially attempts in antiquity to fill in the gaps of the narrative, see John Byron, *Cain and Abel in Text and Tradition: Jewish and Christian Interpretations of the First Sibling Rivalry* (Leiden: Brill, 2011).

3. Byron, *Cain and Abel in Text and Tradition*, 30–31.

4. Von Rad notes that "Every word of this little sentence is difficult: the verb *qānā* ('get,' 'acquire') is just as unusual for the birth of a child as is the use of *īš* ('man') for a newborn boy." Gerhard von Rad, *Genesis: A Commentary* (Philadelphia: The Westminster Press, 1972), 103.

5. Galambush compares Eve's assertive to the man's announcement in Genesis 2:23, "This one was taken out of *'īš*"; now a woman has produced an *'īš*. Julie Galambush, " *'ādām* from *'ādāmâ*, *'iššâ* from *'îš*: Derivation and Subordination in Genesis 2:4b–3:24," in *History and Interpretation: Essays in Honour of John H. Hayes*, ed. M. Patrick Graham, et al. (Sheffield: Sheffield Academic Press, 1993), 33–46 (44). Schneider similarly notes, "The unusual reference to a newly born child as a 'man,' *'ish*, may relate to Eve's ideas about her role in creation." Tammi J. Schneider, *Mothers of Promise: Women in the Book of Genesis* (Grand Rapids: Baker Academic, 2008), 172.

6. Schneider, *Mothers of* Promise, 171–72.

7. E.g., Wenham says that it seems likely that Eve meant, "I have gained a man with the LORD's help." Gordon Wenham, *Genesis 1–15* (Waco: Word Books, 1987), 101–02. Cf. Claus Westermann, *Genesis 1–11: A Commentary*, trans. John J. Scullion (Minneapolis: Augsburg, 1984), 290–91. Many modern translations (including the NRSV, NASB, NIV, ESV, CSB) add the word "help" so that Eve acquired/created Cain with the help of Yhwh. While von Rad also translates the phrase as "with the help of the Lord," he notes that "one must remember that otherwise *'et* never means 'with the help of.'" Von Rad, *Genesis*, 103. Sarna states that the accusative sign *'et* "often has the sense of 'together with,' which supports the addition of the word 'help.'" Nahum M. Sarna, *Genesis: The Traditional Hebrew Text with the New JPS Translation Commentary* (Philadelphia: The Jewish Publication Society, 1989), 32. Alter translates Eve's speech as "I have got me a man with the LORD." Robert Alter, *The Five Books of Moses: A Translation with Commentary* (New York: W.W. Norton & Company, 2004), 29.

8. Marjo C.A. Korpel and Johannes C. de Moor, *Adam, Eve, and the Devil: A New Beginning* (Sheffield: Sheffield Phoenix Press, 2014), 134; Sarna, *Genesis*, 32.

9. Julie Galambush, *Reading Genesis: A Literary and Theological Commentary* (Smyth & Helwys Publishing, 2018), 35. In this, Galambush follows Rosenberg's

translation of "I have created a man as Yahweh has." David Rosenberg and Harold Bloom, *The Book of J* (New York: Grove Weidenfeld, 1990), 187. Galambush, "'*ādām* from '*ādāmâ*,'", 44.

10. Galambush, *Reading Genesis,* 35.

11. Rosenberg, *The Book of J,* 187–88.

12. The word עצב is also used to describe the man's pain/toil in raising crops in Genesis 3:17.

13. Christiana De Groot, "Genesis," in *The IVP Women's Bible* Commentary, eds. Catherine Clark Kroeger and Mary J. Evans (Downers Grove: IVP, 2002), 1–27 (8).

14. Admittedly, Eve's connection to the man Cain remains. Schüngel-Straumann has stated that in Genesis 4 "women do not figure into any of these accounts except as mothers, wives, and daughters of the men named." Helen Schüngel-Straumann, "Genesis 1–11: The Primordial History," in *Feminist Biblical Interpretation: A Compendium of Critical Commentary on the Books of the Bible and Related Literature,* eds. Luise Schottroff and Marie-Theres Wacker (Grand Rapids: Eerdmans, 2012), 1–14 (7).

15. Schneider, *Mothers of Promise,* 174.

16. Carol L. Meyers, Ross S. Kraemer, and Toni Craven, *Women in Scripture: A Dictionary of Named and Unnamed Women in the Hebrew Bible, the Apocryphal/Deuterocanonical Books, and the New Testament* (Grand Rapids: Eerdmans, 2000), 82.

17. Abel may have accidentally (or intuitively) provided the correct offering. Perhaps any offering from the ground would have been unacceptable, due to the fact that the ground Cain works is cursed. Galambush, *Reading Genesis,* 35. Perhaps God is predisposed to favor Abel due to his occupation. Byron, *Cain and Abel in Text and Tradition,* 33. Or it may simply be, as Van Seters suggests, that "the deity in general has a preference for meat over vegetables." John Van Seters, *Prologue to History: The Yahwist as Historian in Genesis* (Louisville: Westminster John Knox, 1992), 137. It may also be that God simply favors younger brothers, a common theme throughout Genesis. Wenham, *Genesis 1–15,* 102. For a discussion of ways in which the MT is elusive on this subject while the LXX has influenced later traditions to view Cain and his offering in negative ways, see Joel N. Lohr, "Genesis 4:1-16 in the Masoretic Text, the Septuagint, and the New Testament," *Catholic Biblical Quarterly* 71 (2009): 485–96.

18. The LXX renders this utterance differently than does the MT, and it can be translated "Have you not sinned if you brought it rightly, but did not rightly divide it?" For an explanation of this translation and a discussion of its implications for interpreters in antiquity, see Byron, *Cain and Abel in Text and Tradition,* 48–56. Byron goes on to discuss the way in which the Hebrew is clear that "sin, as a controlling force, is what seeks to dominate Cain" (57).

19. The LXX contains a directive and commissive in which Cain directs Abel to accompany him out to the field. For a discussion of the ancient translations and ensuing interpretations that fill in the gap here, see Byron, *Cain and Abel in Text and Tradition,* 64–72.

20. John Goldingay, p. 29 of his Introduction to John Rogerson, R. W. L. Moberly, and William Johnstone, *Genesis and Exodus* (Sheffield: Sheffield Academic Press, 2001).

21. David W. Cotter, *Genesis* (Collegeville, MI: The Liturgical Press, 2003), 42.

22. Wenham says that this question "invites Cain to acknowledge his responsibility to his 'brother.'" Wenham, *Genesis 1–15,* 106.

23. Wenham, *Genesis 1–15,* 106.

24. P. Riemann, "Am I My Brother's Keeper?" *Interpretation* 24 (1970): 482–91; John Hartley, *Genesis* (Peabody: Hendrickson, 2000), 83.

25. Cf. Hartley, *Genesis,* 83.

26. Sarna, *Genesis,* 34.

27. Umberto Cassuto, *A Commentary on the Book of Genesis: Part 1—From Adam to Noah, Genesis I–VI8*, trans. Israel Abrahams (Jerusalem: Magnes, 1961), 219. [Italics original]

28. According to Sarna, "Hebrew *'avon* means both sin and its penalty because in the biblical world view the two are inseparable, the latter inhering in the former." Sarna, *Genesis,* 34. Cf. Westermann, *Genesis 1–11*, 309; Wenham, *Genesis 1–15*, 108. For a discussion of the LXX's translation, which adopts a metaphorical interpretation of the Hebrew phrase עון נשא and thus changes Cain's utterance possibly to a request for forgiveness, see Byron, *Cain and Abel in Text and Tradition*, 102.

29. Galambush notes, "In this case, all of humankind are 'family' and obliged to avenge Abel's murder." Galambush, *Reading Genesis,* 37.

30. For a discussion of different options for interpreting Yhwh's utterance that hinge upon potential different uses of the Hebrew word שבעתים, see Byron, *Cain and Abel in Text and Tradition*, 107–19.

31. As Alter notes, "It is of course a mark of protection, not a stigma as the English idiom 'mark of Cain' suggests." Alter, *The Five Books of Moses,* 31.

32. A similar example may be the power of a wedding ring, only after one has performed wedding vows in a marriage ceremony.

33. Allan Boesak, *Black and Reformed: Apartheid, Liberation, and the Calvinist Tradition*, ed. Leonard Sweetman (Maryknoll, NY: Orbis Books, 1984), 137–38.

34. Sarna, *Genesis*, 34.

35. Galambush has noted that the three occupations listed for their descendants do not directly depend upon farming, which corresponds with Cain's curse. Galambush, *Reading Genesis*, 37.

36. E.g., Gordon J. Wenham, *Story as Torah: Reading Old Testament Narrative Ethically* (Grand Rapids: Baker Academic, 2000), 32–33. Cassuto, *Commentary on Genesis*, 243.

37. Schneider, *Mothers of Promise*, 176.

38. Susan Niditch, "Genesis," in *Women's Bible Commentary*, ed. Carol A. Newsom, et al. (Louisville: Westminster John Knox, 2012), 32.

39. Meyers, *Women in Scripture*, 169.

40. Meyers, *Women in Scripture*, 169.

41. Meyers, *Women in Scripture*, 46. Meyers also notes that while no vocational role is ascribed to Naamah, her name comes from the Hebrew root that means "to be

pleasant" or "lovely" and may signify her as "the ancestral singer." Meyers, *Women in Scripture*, 129; cf. Sarna, *Genesis*, 38.

42. Meyers, *Women in Scripture*, 169.

43. Schneider, *Mothers of Promise*, 176.

44. Sarna, *Genesis*, 39.

45. Karolien Vermeulen, "Mind the Gap: Ambiguity in the Story of Cain and Abel," *Journal of Biblical Literature* 133 (2014): 29–42. Vermeulen argues that Abel is not merely a foil for Cain in this story but an important character on whom the text invites reflection.

Chapter 3

A Prayerful Imagination

The Power of "Perhaps" (Gen. 18:16–33; Exod. 32:1–14; Amos 7:1–6)

This chapter seeks to understand the function(s) of questions that appear in biblical intercessory prayers.[1] Some readers may find this topic surprising, as few of us ask God questions when we pray for other people. We may describe for God how we would like the situation to change and perhaps direct God on the details for how to accomplish our desired results. While asking God questions might not occur to us, there are numerous intercessory prayers in the Old Testament that utilize questions.[2]

This investigation will focus on three passages that contain prayers in which an intercessor utilizes questions in petitioning God: (1) Abraham's prayer in Genesis 18:16–33, (2) Moses's prayer in Exodus 32:7–14, and (3) Amos's prayers in Amos 7:1–6.[3] On the story level, it will be shown that the questions in these prayers facilitate the success of the prayer (the perlocutionary act) by directing Yhwh's focus away from negative aspects of the situation and toward aspects of the world to which God is more likely to respond with favor. Operating as directives within the directive, the questions incorporate assertives that utilize what can be called a prayerful imagination, evoking worlds to which God might more easily respond with grace.[4] On the storyteller level, the successful use of the prophet's questions as displayed on the story level invites the audience to consider the perlocutionary power that these questions have upon God. This may not only equip believing audiences to utilize questions in their own prayers but enable them to interact with their world in ways that model God's grace.

ABRAHAM'S PRAYER TO YHWH IN GENESIS 18:16–33

Questions play an important role in the exchange between Yhwh and Abraham concerning the fate of Sodom. The two main parts of this passage (vv. 16–21 and vv. 22–32) display similar speech situations as well as a similarity in structure when the utterances are viewed as speech acts. (See table 3.1.)

Story Level

On the story level, the similarities between Yhwh's invitation and Abraham's intercession may suggest that Abraham constructs his act of intercession upon the way in which Yhwh initiates the conversation. Many interpreters have suggested that Yhwh's speech invites Abraham to become involved in the situation.[5] It is possible that Abraham construes Yhwh's speech to also direct the methodology of his participation.

The opening to Yhwh's speech is of particular interest for the present study, as Yhwh begins by posing a question to the group (consisting of "the men" and Abraham). Yhwh asks, "Shall I hide from Abraham that which I am doing?" (v. 17). Yhwh's question is not a directive for the members of this audience to provide a response, as the ensuing assertives in verses 18–19 clearly answer the question in the negative.[6] Yhwh's hearers are thus directed to think. The non-human hearers, ironically identified as "the men" (הָאֲנָשִׁים), are to redirect their focus, if only briefly, from Sodom (v. 16) to Abraham (v. 17). The question directs Abraham not only to become involved in the conversation but reminds him of the purpose of his election.

The assertives that follow the opening question are that "Abraham will become a great nation, and all the nations of the land shall be blessed in him" (v. 18).[7] Yhwh goes on to indicate that Yhwh has known Abraham so that Abraham may direct his kin to keep the "way of Yhwh," which here is identified as doing "righteousness and justice" (צְדָקָה וּמִשְׁפָּט). By Abraham doing

Table 3.1

Yhwh's Invitation (vv. 16–21)	Abraham's Intercession (vv. 22–32)
Speech situation: "And the men went out from there and they looked toward Sodom; and Abraham was walking with them on their way" (v. 16).	Speech situation: "And the men turned from there and went toward Sodom, and Yahweh remained standing before Abraham" (v. 22).
A. Question: Directive (v. 17)	A. Question: Directive (+ Assertive) (vv. 23–24)
B. Assertives + Directive (vv. 18–19)	B. Assertives + Directive (v. 25)
A' Yhwh's Response: Assertive + Commissive (vv. 20–21)	A' Yhwh's Responses: Commissives (+ Abraham's Assertives) (vv. 26–32)

this, Yhwh will bring about his promise to Abraham. The clear connection of these utterances to the covenant with Abraham may be a reason for why the opening question is not whether Yhwh should reveal these plans to Abraham, but whether Yhwh shall hide them. Abraham is to be involved in Yhwh's dealings in the world, and the way in which he does so specifically involves performing directives on righteousness and justice, the way of Yhwh.

Yhwh then divulges the plan. First, God gives an assertive concerning the greatness of the outcry against Sodom and Gomorrah and the gravity of their sin (v. 20). Then, God issues a commissive by which Yhwh pledges to investigate the matter (v. 21). Many interpreters have assumed that Yhwh is proclaiming judgment and coming destruction against the cities, as if God has already completed the investigation.[8] This would mean that Abraham's intercession involves changing God's mind from that of bringing destruction to showing mercy.[9] However, this view is well-critiqued by interpreters who note that God has only indicated plans to investigate.[10] Indeed, "What I am doing" (v. 17) in God's question corresponds to the commissive, "I must go down and see." (v. 21). Abraham is invited not to change God's mind that has been made up already but to be a part of the decision-making process.

Abraham begins his intercession after the men depart for Sodom, leaving Abraham and Yhwh alone together (v. 22). Abraham utilizes four questions, alternating between a general question and one involving a specific number. The fourth question is actually a continuation (or re-articulation) of the second question (see table 3.2). Lundbom notes that "Yahweh does not answer every question, only those containing specific numbers for saving the city. Neither of the big questions posed at the beginning of the dialogue is answered (vv. 23, 25b)."[11] The general questions do not require an answer; they serve as directives for Yahweh to think. This will impact Yahweh's answers to the specific questions.

The chiastic structure for the broader conversation identified in table 3.1 above can be expanded as shown in table 3.3. The outer framework follows the specific questions through which Abraham questions Yhwh in light of a potential world in which there are fifty righteous in the city (A), and then Yhwh's initial response followed by responses to Abraham subsequently and continuously reducing the number (A'). Abraham's first two questions serve

Table 3.2

Abraham's Questions to Yhwh

General: "Will you sweep away the righteous with the wicked?" (v. 23b)
Specific: "Will you sweep away and not forgive the place for the fifty righteous who are in it?" (v. 24b)
General: "Shall the judge of all the land not do justice?" (v. 25b)
Specific: "Will you destroy the whole city for lack of five?" (v. 28ab)

Table 3.3

Abraham's speech and Yhwh's Responses (vv. 23–32)

A. Abraham's Questions: Directive (+ Assertive) (v. 23–24)
  a. "Will you sweep away the righteous with the wicked?"
    b. Perhaps (אוּלַי) there are fifty righteous within the city;
  a' Will you sweep away and not forgive the place for the fifty righteous who are in it?
    B. Abraham's Assertives (v. 25)
      a. Far be it from you
        b. such a thing: to kill righteous with wicked,
        b' so that the righteous are like the wicked.
      a' Far be it from you
    B' Abraham's Directive (v. 25)
      a. Shall the judge of
        b. all the land
      a' not do justice?
A' Yhwh's Responses: Commissives (+ Abraham's Assertives) (vv. 26–32)
  Yhwh: "If I find in Sodom fifty righteous in the city, I will forgive the whole place for their sake."
  Abraham: (+Behabitive, v. 27) "Perhaps (אוּלַי) five of the fifty are lacking. *Will you destroy the whole city for lack of five?*"
  Yhwh: "I will not destroy it if I find forty-five there."
  Abraham: "Perhaps (אוּלַי) forty are found there."
  Yhwh: "I will not do it for the sake of the forty."
  Abraham: (+Behabitive, v. 30) Perhaps (אוּלַי) thirty are found there.
  Yhwh: I will not do it if I find thirty there.
  Abraham: (+Behabitive, v. 31) Perhaps (אוּלַי) twenty are found there.
  Yhwh: I will not destroy it for the sake of the twenty.
  Abraham: (+Behabitive) Perhaps (אוּלַי) ten are found there.
  Yhwh: I will not destroy it for the sake of the ten.

---

to direct Yhwh to think about how God will act if there are fifty righteous in the city.[12] The illocutionary force of this assertive is impacted by the word *perhaps* (אוּלַי), allowing it to function more like a directive to consider the propositional content than as an assertive, which must be critiqued for its fit with the world.[13] Indeed, the direction of fit for the success of this utterance does not depend upon fitting this world; it must only fit with Abraham's imagination. In fact, neither Abraham nor Yhwh claim to know how many righteous are in the city of Sodom. Earlier, Yhwh had framed the subject of the investigation in terms of the greatness of the outcry and the gravity of the sin of the city; here Abraham is redirecting the search so that the focus is on the righteous in the city.

Before Yhwh responds to Abraham's question concerning the imaginary world, Abraham answers the question. He does so by using the phrase that is often translated "Far be it from you" as an inclusio (a, a') for describing the act of killing the righteous with the wicked (b) and treating the righteous like the wicked (b'). Brueggemann points to the manner in which the first word derives from the term meaning "to pollute" or "defile," so that acting in this way would violate Yahweh's holiness.[14] Abraham continues by asking, "Shall the judge of all the land not do justice?" When taken by itself, this question appears to be ambiguous as it conspicuously lacks צְדָקָה to go with מִשְׁפָּט.[15] However, the question functions along with the previous assertive. As Miller states,

> The appeal of this intercessory prayer is to God's own way of being and acting in the world, the way of justice and righteousness. The question appeals to the character and reputation of God, to press the Lord to be and act according to the divine intention and nature.[16]

It can be noted that the chiasm (B) contains the word צַדִּיק and the chiasm B' concerns מִשְׁפָּט. Abraham's question directs Yhwh to think about Yhwh's own judgment, which is characterized by righteousness (unlike the judgment of earthly kings).[17]

Persuaded, Yhwh responds by issuing a favorable judgment on behalf of the whole city for the sake of the fifty righteous that exist in Abraham's imagination (v. 26). Not yet finished, Abraham continues the conversation by utilizing what speech act theorists call a behabitive, a polite utterance that relies upon societal conventions (v. 27).[18] He then decreases the number of possible righteous in the assertive and restates his question. After Yhwh responds in the same manner as before, Abraham reduces the number four more times, each time using the qualifier *perhaps* and including a behabitive for the final two times. Each time, Yhwh responds in the same way. By reducing the number of righteous in his imaginary city of Sodom and restating his question, Abraham demonstrates that the force of his intercessory question is not in the number of righteous, but the presence of the righteous.

Storyteller Level

On the storyteller level, Yhwh's opening question (vv. 17–18) reminds audiences of God's covenant with Abraham, a recurring theme in Genesis (cf. Gen. 12:1–3; 15:1–21; 17:1–27). Whereas God's question highlights the end result in which he and his descendants are to become a blessing to all of the families of the earth (cf. Gen. 12:1–3), God's answer (v. 19) provides details for how Abraham's people will achieve this purpose by walking in justice and righteousness. This in turn invites audiences to connect with Abraham this dominant theme that appears throughout Scripture, particularly in the prophetic books and in the Psalter.

Abraham's series of repeated questions and Yhwh's repeated responses (with only slight variations) serve to slow down the story and thus focus the audience's attention on this exchange. Unlike the rapid pace of the dialogue in the story immediately preceding this narrative (Gen. 18:1–15), this drawn-out exchange forces the audience to consider Abraham's intercession for the city of Sodom. Furthermore, Abraham's behabitives (v. 27, v. 30aa, v. 31a, 32a) contain references that may remind invite the audience to incorporate or at least consider how this exchange fits with prayers found in the Psalter. For example, Abraham's self-reference as being but "dust and ashes" and the request that God resist from anger fits with Psalm 103, which highlights the limits of God's anger (vv. 9–13) and suggests that divine consideration of humanity being dust and ashes may elicit God's grace (v. 14). Such an intertextual connection is particularly striking, given that many psalms (including Psalm 103) view justice and righteousness to involve oppressors rightly receiving their due punishment. Audiences may be invited to reflect on this tension. On the one hand, the reason for why God is getting involved in Sodom here is to determine the extent of the violence in the city and to bring about justice for the oppressed. On the other hand, God is reluctant to bring about such punishment without considering the impact it may have on the righteous within the city.

On the storyteller level, this entire episode functions as a prequel to the famous story of God destroying Sodom and Gomorrah. A legendary example of God's wrath that resonates throughout Scripture, the story Sodom and Gomorrah is used to convey messages concerning humanity's violence (e.g., Deut. 32:32–33; Jer. 23:14; Ezek. 16:45–49 [46–50]) and of God's punishment (e.g., Deut. 29:21–23 [22–24]; Isa. 1:9–10; 13:19; Jer. 49:18; 50:40; Lam. 4:6; Hos. 11:8–9; Amos 4:11). Placing this story in front of the particular story demonstrates that bringing wrath is not God's preference.[19] In this way, the story itself may function to change the perspective of the audience away from focusing on punishment and toward justice and righteousness, the way of Yhwh.

MOSES'S PRAYER TO YHWH IN EXODUS 32:7–14

Set in the infamous episode regarding the golden calf (Exod. 32:1–35), Yhwh's opening speech to Moses consists of two parts: one describing the situation involving the Israelites' apostasy (vv. 7–9) and the other involving an imaginary world in which Yhwh commits to consuming the Israelites with divine wrath and starting over with Moses (v. 10; see table 3.4). Both sections start with similar directives for Moses to leave. However, as perlocutionary acts, they function in an ironic way: Moses stays and becomes involved. As

Table 3.4

Yhwh's Speech (vv. 7b–10)	*Moses's Speech (vv. 11b–13)*
A. Directive ("Go down at once") (v. 7ba)	A. Directive (Question) (v. 11ba)
B. Assertives concerning present situation (vv. 7bb–9)	B. Assertives concerning present situation (vv. 11bb–11bc)
a. Description of Israelites ("your people")	a. Description of Israelites ("your people")
b. Summary and description of their apostasy	b. Summary of God's actions
a' Description of Israelites as stubborn	
A' Directive ("Now, leave me alone") (v. 10aa)	A' Directive (Question) (v. 12aa)
B' Commissives (v. 10ab–10b)	B. Assertives (world-from-words) of resulting Egyptian speech (v. 12ab)
a. Yhwh's wrath against the Israelites	A. Directives (12b–13)
b. Yhwh's promise to Moses	a. Yhwh's wrath against the Israelites
	b. Yhwh's promise to Abraham

Childs has famously noted, Yhwh's second directive ("Leave me alone") operates paradoxically as an invitation that opens up the possibility of intercession in a manner similar to that made by Abraham.[20]

Story Level

Moses begins his response to Yahweh with two questions (v. 11b–12a), each starting with "Why?" (לָמָה). These questions are clearly not intended as requests for information; if so, then the first question of why Yhwh's wrath burns against Yhwh's people is positioned immediately after the answer has been given! But as directives to think, these questions invite Yhwh to consider aspects of the situation that differ from the focus of Yhwh's opening speech.

Interpreters have noticed the way Moses uses his first question to counter Yhwh's designation of the Israelites as "your [Moses's] people" and to point out that it was Yhwh who brought them out of Egypt.[21] The Israelites are Yhwh's covenant people. Conspicuously, Moses then offers no assertive regarding the present actions of the Israelites. He removes that aspect of Yhwh's speech and replaces it with the question, "Why should the Egyptians say, 'With evil (בְּרָעָה) he brought them out, to kill them in the mountains to consume them from the face of the earth'?" This directive utilizes a prayerful imagination, as its accompanying assertive is similar to those offered by Abraham concerning the righteous in Sodom. Unlike Abraham, Moses does not utilize the qualifier, *perhaps* in the world he creates with his words. Instead, he utilizes Yhwh's own description of the intended action to "consume" the Israelites and imagines how this will be construed by the Egyptians. Thus, Moses uses his second question to direct Yhwh to think about Yhwh's reputation rather than the Israelites' transgression, an approach similar to his intercession in Numbers 14:13–25. The force of such an appeal to Yhwh is not based on divine vanity[22] but is tied to God's purpose in the world.[23] Bruckner states that "the sin of the people had put the reputation of the Lord's salvation at risk."[24] But Moses invites Yhwh to consider that Yhwh's reputation will only be damaged if God acts out of anger.

Storyteller Level

Many interpreters are shocked by Yhwh's opening speech in this story, and they struggle against the opening divine speech because it challenges their own perspective of God. Some suggest that God must not be sincere but rather is testing Moses, thus maintaining their view of God's sovereignty and immutability. Others have dismissed the entire episode as a later redaction that is not to be taken seriously. Such resistance by the audience on the storyteller level fits well with Moses's resistance on the story level, particularly in the way in which Moses is concerned with how Yhwh's speech acts might impact Yhwh's reputation.

Eliciting shock at how God acts in the golden calf narrative is an intentional feature on the storyteller level, one that is crucial in both the illocutionary and perlocutionary function of this story. Yhwh's extreme adverse response upon seeing the Israelites make an image to represent God provides ancient audiences a powerful reinforcement to the earlier prohibition against making an idol and utilizing it in their worship of Yhwh (Exod. 20:4–6). Such a message is enforced further when Moses, after successfully interceding for the Israelites, cannot restrain himself from punishing the Israelites when he sees the golden calf with his own eyes (Exod. 32:19–29). The story thus serves as an illocutionary act to buttress the commandment against idolatry (illocutionary act) in order to discourage the Israelites from ever breaking this commandment again (perlocutionary act).[25] For modern audiences, the way in which Moses points to Yhwh's covenant and reputation in connection to the relationship to God's people, as opposed to God's omniscience and immutability, may challenge interpreters to consider their own assumptions about what might motivate God to act. Many modern interpreters, especially Christians, have ignored ways in which God is depicted throughout Scripture as a relational Being and replaced that view of God with a stoic and logical depictions of God that stem more from their own traditions. In this way, the storyteller level resists the idolatry of both ancient and modern interpreters.

The storyteller level also invites intertextual conversations. Audiences who are familiar with the flood story in Genesis might notice a similar pattern with this episode in that God is quick to consider starting over after seeing how humans disregard God's intentions for them. The flood story famously uses the root נחם in reference to God (Gen. 6:6–7), and Moses's prayer here is the next time in the larger narrative in which נחם is used in reference to God.[26] Indeed, Moses's prayer is the first of many passages in Scripture that discuss the key characteristic of God as sometimes who might have a change of mind (e.g., Judg. 2:18; 1 Sam. 15:11, 35; 2 Sam. 24:15–16; incl. when asked or in light of repentance, e.g., Jer. 18:1–12; Amos 7:1–6; Jon. 3:9–10; 4:2), but not always doing so (e.g., Num. 23:19–20; 1 Sam. 15:29; Jer. 4:28).[27]

When viewed in the context of intercessory prayer, Moses's prayer opens up the possibility of humans interceding even when it appears that God has made a decision, as opposed to Abraham's intercessory prayer that occurred in the process of God coming to a decision. In particular, the power of alluding to God's covenant and God's reputation are presented as effective in praying to God. Such themes are prevalent in prayers found in the Psalter that ask God for grace in the face of exile. Overall, Moses's prayer invites audiences to imagine that God is someone to whom they can approach, even when it seems to be too late.

AMOS'S PRAYERS TO YHWH IN AMOS 7:1–6

Whereas most of the book of Amos directs God's message of judgment against the northern kingdom of Israel, two intercessory prayers by Amos for the nation appear in Amos 7:1–6 (see table 3.5).

Story Level

The two prayers are brief and nearly identical, although the situations differ in the type and scope of calamity facing Israel. The first prayer includes a

Table 3.5

Amos's First Plea (v. 2b)	Amos's Second Plea (v. 5b)
Speech situation: vision of the Lord Yhwh forming locusts that ate up the grass of the land.	*Speech situation*: vision of the Lord Yhwh calling to contend by fire, which devoured the great deep and was devouring the plot [of land].
Expressive ("O Lord Yhwh")	Expressive ("O Lord Yhwh")
Directive ("Please forgive")	Directive ("Please cease")
Directive ("How can Jacob stand?")	Directive ("How can Jacob stand?")
Assertive ("He is so small!")	Assertive ("He is so small!")

wide-sweeping request to forgive (v. 2b) whereas the second request asks Yhwh to stop (v. 5b). For both, Amos utilizes the same question ("How can Jacob stand?"), followed by the same assertive, "He is so small." Unlike Moses, Amos does not explicitly ask Yhwh to have a change of mind (נחם). In both cases, the result is (nearly) identical, with Yhwh having a change of mind (נִחַם יהוה עַל־זֹאת) and issuing a declarative that prevents the vision from occurring (vv. 3, 6).

While there are differences in Amos's argument when compared to the intercession of Abraham and Moses (most conspicuously in length but also in content),[28] the function of the questions remains consistent. As in the prayers of Abraham and Moses, the question functions as a directive to think about the situation according to the prayerful imagination of the prophet. Interpreters have noticed that this prayer appeals to God's nature, including Yhwh's mercy and tendency to side with the weak. Calling the nation by the name Jacob also directs Yhwh to consider the beginnings of God's relationship with this people. When followed by the assertive ("He is so small!") the question also functions as an indirect assertive that presents a case that Israel will not survive the punishment. Apparently, Amos does not think that he must direct Yhwh here to think about God's justice (so Abraham) or God's covenant and reputation (so Moses). Perhaps then Yhwh's mercy will work on its own (cf. the way in which Yhwh's compassion leads God to act mercifully after Yhwh asks questions in Hosea 11:8–9).

Following these two visions are two more visions (Amos 7:7–9; 8:1–3) that are separated by a narrative (Amos 7:10–17). Both of these visions include an opening question by God to Amos, asking him what he sees. While interpreters have wrestled with identifying how exactly the two objects presented by Yhwh relate to their respective judgments—especially the first object of the "plumb line" (אֲנָךְ)—it can be observed that after Amos declares what he sees, he does not protest, suggesting that what he sees has influenced his perspective.[29]

Storyteller Level

On the storyteller level, an audience might note intertextual connections with both of Amos's directives for Yhwh to "please forgive" (סְלַח־נָא) and to "please cease" (חֲדַל־נָא). For example, forgiveness can be result of priestly actions, as it is in Leviticus (e.g., Lev. 4:20, 26, 31, 35), can be given after an act of repentance (e.g., Isa. 55:7), and as in this passage, can simply be granted by Yhwh upon request without any accompanying sacrifice or repentance (e.g., Num. 14:19–20). The request for Yhwh to "cease" (חדל) might be compared to how Yhwh ceases the punishment of thunder and hail against Egypt upon Pharaoh's request and Moses's prayer (Exod. 9:27–33).

The repetition of Amos's prayer as the exact same response to both visions may highlight the effectiveness of asking God to consider the small size and weakness of God's people, as well as to demonstrate God's reluctance to bring such devastation upon them. This feature of the passage, coupled with the placement of these visions before the ones in which God does not withhold the punishment (Amos 7:7–9; 8:1–3), may thus function in a way that is similar to the repetition and placement of Abraham's intercession for the city of Sodom. The audience may also note that in the two visions that follow (Amos 7:7–9; 8:1–3), it is Yhwh who asks Amos a question. The fact that Amos does not ask God to refrain from the punishment in these last two visions suggests that questions may hold the power of persuasion.

CONCLUSIONS

Patrick Miller suggests that the primary intent of the great intercessors in the Old Testament is "to divert the divine anger [from] the sin of the people, as, for example, Abraham does for Sodom and Gomorrah, Moses for the sinful community in the wilderness, Amos for the sins of the Northern Kingdom."[30] The present study agrees with this assessment but notes that in all three cases this act of diverting God's anger is one that is prompted by God. Miller goes on to identify the function of motive clauses within these prayers: "In the broadest sort of way, they tend either to draw attention to some feature of God's *nature and character* or to lift up some aspect of *the situation of the petitioner(s)*."[31] The present study suggests that it is the questions in these intercessory prayers that contribute to the aim identified by Miller.

By asking God questions, the intercessor directs Yhwh to think about the situation in ways that guide Yhwh to respond favorably to the petition. Abraham uses his questions to participate in Yhwh's decision concerning Sodom by directing Yhwh's attention to the (possible) righteous rather than the wicked people in Sodom. Moses uses questions to direct Yhwh's focus away from the people's apostasy and toward Yhwh's covenant with them. In addition, by his questions, Moses guides Yhwh to consider one outcome of proceeding with the decision to destroy the Israelites and start over with Moses. Amos uses one question in two prayers to direct Yhwh to consider the frailty of God's people and thus the need for Yhwh to forgive and to cease. In each of these cases, the intercessor prays in response to God's prompting, which suggests that God invites the opportunity to think about aspects of these situations in ways that will lead God to respond favorably to the intercessor. The prophets do not engage in acts of manipulation of God but of joining with God.[32]

The questions within the intercessory prayers do not simply influence God but can influence the listening audience in at least two ways. First, the intercessory prayers in these texts might challenge us to incorporate questions as we pray for others. We might try asking God to consider aspects of their situation that fit with God's purposes for the world and for God's people. In addition to strengthening the force of our prayer, such an act would also serve to remind both us and our communities of God's grace and our mission to the world that God so loves. It also might encourage us to become more familiar with the situation facing the person or group for whom we are praying. Asking God questions in these prayers has the potential to strengthen our prayers as well as our relationship with God and each other.

Second, the questions in these prayers might also transform our own imaginations. With Abraham, we might imagine that sin doesn't automatically have the final word, even in our fallen world. We might be encouraged to live in this world, knowing that the presence of the righteous fosters a hope for repentance and redemption in the world (cf. Jesus speaking of God's people as the salt and light of the world in Matt. 5:13–16). Admittedly, we would also acknowledge that there is eventually a time for God's judgment against the world. With Moses and Amos, we might see a hope of God giving God's people second and third chances, achieving divine purposes even when God's people fall short. Admittedly, we would also be aware, with Moses and Amos, that there is a time for God's judgment against God's people. These prayers do more than teach us how to pray, they can teach us how to live as God's people. The questions in these intercessory prayers might at times redirect our focus away from a purely judgmental attitude to one that first remembers, and appeals to, the gracious character of God.

NOTES

1. Previous versions of this paper have been published as Steven Mann, "Ask and You Shall Intercede: The Peculiar Perlocutionary Power of Asking God Questions," *Bulletin for Biblical Research* 29.2 (2019): 208–24, and Steven T. Mann, "Ask and You Shall Intercede: The Power of a Prayerful Imagination," in *Speaking with God: Probing Old Testament Prayers for Contemporary Significance*, eds. Phillip Camp and Elaine Phillips (McMaster Divinity College Press, 2021), 154–71. Used by permission.

2. There are also Scripture passages that display intercessory prayers that do not utilize questions, so this chapter does not suggest that questions are always necessary in such prayers.

3. The selected texts are intended to serve as a sample of intercessory prayers that utilize questions as opposed to a complete list.

4. I am borrowing the term "prayerful imagination" from Phillip G. Camp, "Prayer in the Pentateuch," in *Praying with Ancient Israel Exploring the Theology of Prayer in the Old Testament*, eds. Phillip G. Camp and Tremper Longman III (Abilene: Abilene Christian University Press, 2015), 21–36 (31). Camp uses the term to denote an aspect of God's creative activity, specifically the way in which prayer "opens one's eyes to the power of God and the future God is creating." I will use the term as a way to describe the ways in which an intercessor can utilize a world-from-words direction of fit that can open God's eyes to possible aspects of the speech situation.

5. E.g., John Goldingay, *Old Testament Theology: Volume Three: Israel's Life* (Downers Grove: InterVarsity Press, 2009), 267–68; Robert B. Chisholm Jr., "Anatomy of an Anthropomorphism: Does God Discover Facts?" *Bibliotheca Sacra* 164 (2007): 3–20 (8); Terence Fretheim, *The Suffering of God: An Old Testament Perspective* (Philadelphia: Fortress Press, 1984), 49–50.

6. In recognition of this the NRSV adds the word "No" at the beginning of verse 19.

7. I take Genesis 18:18 as an indicative (so also NIV, CSB, NET), but even if it continues the interrogative of Genesis 18:17 (NRSV, NKJV, NASB) it nevertheless functions as an assertive that justifies the question.

8. For a helpful overview of this prevailing viewpoint, see Nathan MacDonald, "Listening to Abraham—Listening to Yhwh: Divine Justice and Mercy in Genesis 18:16-33," *Catholic Biblical Quarterly* 66 (2004): 25–43 (28–30).

9. E.g., Ben Zvi states, "The conclusion to which Abraham's argument leads is clear from the onset: God should change his/her plans concerning Sodom . . ." Ehud Ben Zvi, "The Dialogue Between Abraham and YHWH in Gen 18:23–32: A Historical-Critical Analysis," *Journal for the Study of the Old Testament* 17 (1992): 27–46 (33).

10. E.g., William John Lyons, *Canon and Exegesis: Canonical Praxis and the Sodom Narrative* (London: Sheffield Academic Press, 2002), 174–76; MacDonald, "Listening to Abraham," 29.

11. Jack R. Lundbom, "Parataxis, Rhetorical Structure, and the Dialogue Over Sodom in Genesis 18," in *The World of Genesis: Persons, Places, Perspectives*, eds. Philip R. Davies and David J. A. Clines (Sheffield: Sheffield Academic Press, 1998), 136–45 (141).

12. Interpreters are divided on whether Abraham is interceding for the entire city or only for the righteous. For a discussion of this topic, see Lyons, *Canon and Exegesis*, 197–202.

13. Cf. the translation for אוּלַי here in the NRSV and NASB as "suppose."

14. Walter Brueggemann, *Great Prayers of the Old Testament* (Louisville: Westminster John Knox, 2008), 5–6. Brueggemann points out that the term "holiness" (קֹדֶשׁ) is the antithesis of the term "profane" (חֹל).

15. Lyons states:

[T]he rhetorical question, 'shall not the Judge of all the earth do justice' [is] deeply ambiguous. Obviously, YHWH is that judge (cf. vv. 20–21) and it is, so Abraham believes, unthinkable that the deity should act unjustly. But it is not clear what Abraham now considers justice to be. (Lyons, *Canon and Exegesis,* 193)

MacDonald suggests that Abraham "did not rightly understand Yhwh" and points to his omission of "righteousness" as evidence. MacDonald goes on to suggest that Abraham is concerned with judicial procedure. MacDonald, "Listening to Abraham," 37.

16. Patrick D. Miller, *They Cried to the Lord: The Form and Theology of Biblical Prayer* (Minneapolis: Fortress Press, 1994), 116–18, 269.

17. For a description of a human king's *mishpat,* see 1 Samuel 8:11–17.

18. A behabitive is an utterance that relies upon societal conventions, including speeches made with the intention of being polite. Austin, *How To Do Things With Words,* 152. For a study on the politeness of Abraham's intercession, see Edward Bridge, "Abraham's Dialogue with God in Genesis 18," *Journal for the Study of the Old Testament* 40 (2016): 281–96.

19. Commenting on the description of God bringing destruction as "strange" and "alien" in Isaiah 28:21, John Goldingay suggests that bringing destruction is not central to Yhwh's character. "While this task [of bringing destruction on Judah] is clearly alien to Yahweh's ultimate nature and purpose, it will be done if necessary as a means to that purpose's fulfillment." John Goldingay, *Isaiah* (Understanding the Bible Commentary Series; Grand Rapids: Baker Books, 2001), 15.

20. Brevard Childs, *The Book of Exodus* (Louisville: The Westminster Press, 1974), 567. Cf. Camp, "Prayer in the Pentateuch," 27.

21. Camp, "Prayer in the Pentateuch," 28.

22. Against William H.C. Propp, *Exodus 19–40* (New York: Doubleday, 2006), 555.

23. Cf. Miller, *They Cried to the Lord,* 272.

24. James K. Bruckner, *Exodus* (Peabody, MA: Hendrickson, 2008), 284–85.

25. From this perspective, this story operates alongside Exodus 20:4–6 in a way that is similar to how the book of Jonah might illustrate the message found in Jeremiah 18:1–11.

26. The root is used with human references in regard to Noah (Gen. 5:29), Esau (Gen. 27:42), Jacob (Gen. 37:35), Judah (Gen. 38:12), Joseph and his brothers (Gen. 50:21), and the Israelites (Exod. 13:17).

27. For a helpful study on this recurring theme in Scripture, see David Noel Freedman, "When God Repents," in *Divine Commitment and Human Obligation: Selected Writings of David Noel Freedman,* ed. John R. Huddlestun (Grand Rapids: Eerdmans, 1997), 409–46.

28. E.g., Shalom Paul notes that in these prayers Amos "does not call upon the traditional guarantees of salvation, nor does he cite the Lord's promises to the patriarchs. The prayer, moreover, is not even motivated by a reminder of Israel's election." Paul goes on to point out that for Amos, Israel's election is actually connected to the punishment (Amos 3:2). Shalom M. Paul, *Amos* (Minneapolis: Fortress Press, 1991), 229.

29. When comparing the two visions, it is clearer what the final vision, that of the summer fruit (קַיִץ), has to do with the message of judgment, as the relation between "summer fruit" (קַיִץ) and "the end" (הַקֵּץ) appears to function as a pun that highlights

the punishment. It is less certain what showing Amos a "plumb line" has to do with the ensuing message of judgment against Israel's places of worship and against the house of Jeroboam.

30. Miller, *They Cried to the Lord*, 90.

31. Miller, *They Cried to the Lord*, 116 [italics original].

32. Cf. Camp, who says that "prayer is no way manipulates or forces God to act. Though prayer is relational, it is not a relationship of equals." Camp, "Prayer in the Pentateuch," 29.

Chapter 4

Predatory and Protective Worlds in Exodus 1:8–22

After exploring ways in which words can create worlds that clash with one another (chapter 2), and seeing that these worlds-from-words can be used to impact divine decisions in intercessory prayer (chapter 3), we now turn our attention to investigating ways in which characters can use their narrative worlds to both prey upon and protect others. In biblical stories, it is often (but not always) kings who use their words to oppress others, and it is often (but not always) quick-thinking women who are aligned with Yhwh and save the oppressed by creating worlds with their words.[1] One story stands out and serves as a case study for this phenomenon: the story of Pharaoh and the midwives in Exodus 1:8–22. On the story level, both Pharaoh and the midwives perform assertives that portray their world in ways that can help them achieve their respective (and opposing) goals. Ironically, these worlds overlap, as the midwives resist Pharaoh's aim of killing Hebrew boys by appealing to an aspect of the imaginary world that is cast by Pharaoh's own words. On the storyteller level, Shiphrah and Puah's brave deeds foreshadow the coming conflict between Pharaoh and Yhwh (and Moses) while also providing a practical example for putting their fear of God in action. This story also participates in important thematic conversations, such as resisting the toxic imagination of oppressors, and engages in numerous intertextual conversations throughout Scripture.

The opening chapter of the book of Exodus is dominated by speech acts delivered by the king of Egypt, first to his people (vv. 9–10), then to the Hebrew midwives (vv. 16, 18b), and then again to his people (v. 22b). The directives to the midwives and their ensuing response to the king (v. 19) are central to this passage in both structure and content (see table 4.1).

Table 4.1

Verse	Speaker	Hearer(s)	Illocutionary Act(s)	Responses/Results to Perlocutionary Act(s)
vv. 9–10	a new king over Egypt	his people	assertive directive assertive	Response (intended): The hearers perform intended oppressive actions Result (unintended): An intensification of the original situation
v. 16	the king of Egypt	Hebrew midwives, Shiphrah and Puah	directives	Response (unintended): The hearers do not follow the king's directives but instead act according to their fear of God Result: Confrontation with the king of Egypt.
v. 18	the king of Egypt	the midwives	directive	Response (intended): the midwives respond
v. 19	the midwives	Pharaoh	assertives	Results: God deals well with the midwives, and the original situation with the people continues
v. 22	Pharaoh	all his people	directives	Response: Not specified Results: Not specified (but lead into the ensuing story of the birth of Moses)

Story Level

The narrator sets the scene for this story by providing an overview of the names of the sons of Israel who came to Egypt and joined Joseph (vv. 1–5), sharing that these characters and their whole generation have died (v. 6), and then stating that the Israelites have dramatically increased in both number and in strength (v. 7). The narrator then introduces the first character to speak in the book of Exodus, a new king of Egypt who does not know Joseph and thus cannot be expected to act in faithfulness to Joseph's people (v. 8).[2] All of the king's illocutionary acts attempt (and fail) to achieve the same perlocutionary act, that of reducing the number and strength of the Israelite people.

The king's opening speech consists of an assertive, a directive, and then another assertive (see table 4.2). The assertives create a world that provides a foundation for the directive. He begins the first assertive with the particle הִנֵּה ("here"), a word commonly used in biblical narrative to direct attention

Table 4.2

(Directed) Assertive	הִנֵּה עַם בְּנֵי יִשְׂרָאֵל רַב וְעָצוּם מִמֶּנּוּ	Here, the people of the Israelites are more numerous and more powerful than us.
Directive	הָבָה נִתְחַכְּמָה לוֹ	Come, let us act wisely with them,
Assertive	פֶּן־יִרְבֶּה וְהָיָה כִּי־תִקְרֶאנָה מִלְחָמָה וְנוֹסַף גַּם־הוּא עַל־שֹׂנְאֵינוּ וְנִלְחַם־בָּנוּ וְעָלָה מִן־הָאָרֶץ׃	lest they increase and when a battle happens, they will be added to our enemies and they will fight against us, and they will go up from the land.

to an element in the story.[3] In this case, the king's assertive that the Israelites as "more numerous and powerful" than his people (רַב וְעָצוּם מִמֶּנּוּ) fits with the narrative world as depicted by the narrator, who used the same words to describe the Israelites (see v. 7). However, unlike the narrator's use of plural verbal forms of רָבָה and עָצַם for the Israelites (וַיִּרְבּוּ וַיַּעַצְמוּ), the king here uses the collective singular nouns to contrast "the people of the Israelites" from "us." This "us versus them" portrayal of the narrative world dehumanizes the Israelites as a collective without concern for the impact upon individuals or families.

This dehumanized depiction of the Israelites in the king's opening assertive leads into the king's main directive to "come" (הָבָה) and "let us act wisely with them" (נִתְחַכְּמָה לוֹ, v. 10a). This directive utilizes a theme often found in wisdom settings that is especially prevalent in a royal courtly setting. When taken by itself, an audience might feel a need to request further direction on how specifically wisdom might be used. But when uttered after the assertives that describe the number and power of the Israelite people, the directive will likely be construed as instructions to deal with this aspect of this group and reduce their number and power. Indeed, any question that the king intends this perlocutionary act with his words is removed with the assertives that follow his directive.

Unlike his opening assertive that depends upon what can be observed for its match with the world as it was described by the narrator, the assertives that follow the directive depend only upon the king's imagination. In a manner that is similar to Abraham's use of "perhaps" in Genesis 18, the king uses "lest" (פֶּן) to evoke a world in which a hypothetical battle or war occurs. According to the king, in such a situation the growing Israelite group will side with Egypt's enemies (whomever they may be), fight against the Egyptians, and then go up out of the land (v. 10). A projected scenario based solely on the king of Egypt's imagination, these assertives function indirectly as directives for the Egyptians to view the Israelite people as both a threat to be feared and a resource to be exploited. The king thus starts with assertives that match the narrative world, and then support his directive by offering assertives that only match the world that he creates with his words.

The king's people respond with actions that correspond to Pharaoh's imagined world of fear and exploitation that is on display in the royal assertives and create a system of oppression that results in coercing the Israelite people to build supply cities for Pharaoh (Pithom and Rameses, see v. 11). While this result may be viewed as a success when viewing the group as a resource to be managed and exploited, the main perlocutionary act, the reduction of the number of the Israelites, is unfulfilled. Moreover, the opposite of Pharaoh's perlocutionary act occurs as the numbers of the Israelite people actually increase (v. 12a)! This situation, along with Pharaoh's created world in the minds of the Egyptians, continues to fuel the Egyptians' fear of the Israelites as they increase their violent exploitation (v. 12b–14).

After the initial failure to limit the number and strength of the Israelite people, the king of Egypt tries again (see table 4.3). Whereas the king previously had experienced some initial success in achieving the desired response of his audience (albeit not in the overall aim), this time the audience does not respond as the king intends. Another difference can be seen in the way this audience is described: unlike the general audience of the previous scene, who are identified by their connection to the king as "his people" (עַמּוֹ), this smaller audience are both named and are described as "the Hebrew midwives" (v. 15). The precise connection of these women to the Hebrews is unclear, as their names may or may not indicate that they are Hebrew. Similarly, there is ambiguity in regard to their designation, as it could include them as belonging to the Hebrew community or simply tasked with serving the Hebrew women.[4] Either way, these women are described in connection

Table 4.3

Speaker	Speech		Speech Act
The king of Egypt (v. 16)	בְּיַלֶּדְכֶן אֶת־הָעִבְרִיּוֹת וּרְאִיתֶן עַל־הָאָבְנָיִם	In your helping of the Hebrew women to give birth, look at the stones.	Directive
	אִם־בֵּן הוּא וַהֲמִתֶּן אֹתוֹ	If it is a son, put him to death.	Directive
	וְאִם־בַּת הִיא וָחָיָה:	If it is a daughter, she may live.	Directive
The king of Egypt (v. 18b)	מַדּוּעַ עֲשִׂיתֶן הַדָּבָר הַזֶּה וַתְּחַיֶּיןָ אֶת־הַיְלָדִים:	Why have you done this thing and let the boys live?	Directive
The midwives (v. 19ab–19b)	כִּי לֹא כַנָּשִׁים הַמִּצְרִיֹּת הָעִבְרִיֹּת כִּי־חָיוֹת	Because the Hebrew women are not like the Egyptian women, because they are lively.	Assertive
	הֵנָּה בְּטֶרֶם תָּבוֹא אֲלֵהֶן הַמְיַלֶּדֶת וְיָלָדוּ:	Here, before the midwife comes to them, they give birth.	Assertive

with the Hebrews and their own personhood, rather than by their allegiance to the king.

The king issues three directives that function together as consecutive steps in the larger perlocutionary act of reducing the number of the Hebrew population. The opening directive offers both a general description of the midwives' work ("In your helping of the Hebrew women to give birth") and a narrow directive that specifies one aspect of that work ("look at the stones"). Translations render this directive in different ways, depending on the interpreter's construal of whether the king is using the word stones literally (as bricks) or figuratively (as testicles).[5] While the latter translation is preferred in the present interpretation, in both views the king points to a specific aspect of the midwives' work, which then leads into his ensuing directives. Each of these are presented with "if" (אִם), indicating a potential situation that is followed by the directive for that circumstance. The king directs the midwives to put a male infant to death but to refrain from killing a female infant. Such actions, if performed as the king directs, would conceivably reduce the Hebrew population.

Shiphrah and Puah do not act as they are directed by the king and thus, his perlocutionary act fails. The narrator describes their actions, first that they feared God, then that "they did not do as the king of Egypt spoke to them," and finally that "they let the boys live" (v. 17).

The king responds by summoning the midwives and issuing one more directive, a question that directs them to respond. Notably, this question incorporates only two of the three components of the midwives' actions as previously described by the narrator. He asks, "Why have you done this and let the boys live?" While the second and third descriptions of the midwives' actions appear in the narrator's description, the first description, which involves their motivation (i.e., they feared God), is conspicuously missing. Given the pattern on display that shows similarities between the narrator's assertives and the king's directive, the audience might expect the midwives to respond by filling in this component and say something like, "We did this and allowed the boys to live because we fear God." The midwives choose a different approach when responding to the king.

While the true motivation for the midwives' actions is highlighted on the storyteller level (see below), on the story level they conceal this reason by offering Pharaoh assertives that fit with Pharaoh's toxic imagination. They use the world that was created from Pharaoh's own words against him. Building upon the divisive picture of the Hebrew people offered earlier by the king, the midwives allege an inherent difference between the Hebrew women and Egyptian women in that the former are "lively" (חָיוֹת). This leads to their main assertive and the response proper to the Pharaoh's question, that the Hebrew women give birth before a midwife can get to them (v. 19). As the king had done earlier in portraying the world to his people, the midwives present this claim by using "here" (הֵנָּה), thus inviting the king to see an aspect of the world that is created by their words. As Gafney says, the midwives "use the pharaoh's cultural bias against him" as they essentially say, "The Hebrew women are brutish, animalistic, *chayoth*–not refined, like Egyptian women. Their babies just plop out of them."[6] Gafney goes on to point out, "The word *chayoth* occurs only in this place. However, it is a homophone for and likely related to the noun *chayah,* 'wild animal.'"[7] Similarly, Frymer-Kensky calls the designation an "ethnic slur" and points out that the midwives are "building on the fact that Pharaoh sees Israel as 'other.'"[8] These assertives do not match the world as it is described by the narrator, but they do fit with a world in which the Hebrew people are dehumanized by Pharaoh and feared because of their strength. The midwives thus turn this fear against Pharaoh to frustrate his main perlocutionary act, that of limiting the number and strength of the Hebrew people.

It may seem to Pharaoh that his last directive to the midwives has succeeded. After all, his directive had instructed them to provide the reason for why they had allowed the Hebrew sons to live; the midwives' response is construed to be satisfactory, and Pharaoh has no follow-up questions. Instead, the narrator shares how God responds to the midwives' actions, a significant statement on the storyteller level (see below), and describes how the Israelite people continue to grow more numerous and powerful (vv. 20–21). Despite all of the king's oppressive directives, the initial situation regarding the number and strength of the Israelites has only intensified.

Pharaoh does not give up. The scene closes with Pharaoh issuing to "all his people" a variation of the directive he had given to the midwives, to "throw every son into the Nile, but to let every daughter live" (v. 22). Such a response suggests that Pharaoh believes the midwives' claim as he continues with his strategic plan in a general way but removes them as participants and extends the time period in which the Hebrew male babies are to be killed. Strangely, Pharaoh does not actually clarify that only the Hebrew sons should be thrown into the Nile. While many translations add this detail (e.g., NRSV, NIV, ESV), it is possible that Pharaoh assumes that such a distinction is unnecessary in light of his earlier speech acts. Pharaoh may trust that his people, the Egyptians, will understand this directive to be a continuation of his prior efforts against the Israelite population (see vv. 9–14). It is also possible that Pharaoh believes that "all" his people include the Hebrew women themselves. Whether or not they belong in this category remains to be seen.

Storyteller Level

When viewed on the storyteller level, this story connects with key elements of both the past and future in the overall narrative. An audience who is aware of Yhwh's earlier covenant with the Israelite people is alerted to the way in which the three references in this passage to their increased numerical growth (vv. 9, 12, 20) signals divine blessing in the context of the covenant God made with Abraham (e.g., see Gen. 12:1–3; 15:1–6; 18:17–19). The evidence of God's blessing the Israelites is viewed as a threat by the king of Egypt, placing this human king in opposition to God's plans. As Sarna states, "Pharaoh now unwittingly challenges the will of God, for the divine promise to Abraham had pledged that his descendants would be as numerous as the stars of the heaven and the sands of the seashore."[9] This story also holds connections to the end of Genesis as it explains the way in which the servitude of the Israelites to Pharaoh, initiated earlier by Joseph to save his family from the famine (Gen. 47), becomes an unbearable situation of harsh oppression.

Looking forward, this story opens a new chapter in Israel's saga by highlighting the ascension of an Egyptian king who is not committed to Joseph. Viewing the Israelites both as a threat to be overcome as well as a commodity to be managed, the toxic imagination of this Egyptian king foreshadows the contest that the next Pharaoh will have with Yhwh and Moses. This is shown not only by the way in which the king attempts to quell the results of God's covenant with the Israelites but also by the way in which the midwives' resistance of Pharaoh is portrayed as an outworking of fearing God. The Egyptian king's preoccupation with killing all Hebrew males at birth may also be construed as an (unwitting) attempt to block the birth of Moses; this story sets the context for the story of the birth of Israel's leader (Exod. 2). Ultimately, this story shows that Pharaoh and Yhwh are on a collision course in which only one of them can prevail.

Thematically, this conflict between Pharaoh and Yhwh extends throughout Scripture and even transcends textual boundaries by reflecting aspects of the audience's own world. As Brueggemann states, "The narrative of the Exodus is designed to show the radical criticism and radical delegitimizing of the Egyptian empire."[10] Throughout his prolific writings, Brueggemann has consistently and persuasively articulated ways in which the "royal consciousness" of the dominant culture, represented by Pharaoh in his cruel coercion, relentlessly works to oppose to the alternative community that is represented in Scripture by Moses and is marked by neighborliness.[11] Those operating with the royal consciousness seek to maintain the status quo and typically display a fascination with wisdom, while ignoring the cries of those who are being crushed by the system.[12] For Brueggemann, Pharaoh is a paradigm for every totalizing regime that "monopolizes both technology and imagination, and that will allow no voice that contradicts the claims and power of the prevailing ideology."[13] Brueggemann calls the Exodus story a symbol that "above all, is turned to show for all would-be pharaohs that Exodus is a catastrophic ending of what had seemed forever."[14] Scripture's testimony of ancient Israel's escape from Pharaoh and their covenantal life with Yhwh functions as a reminder that all totalizing regimes are temporary.

As a prequel to the Exodus story, this short narrative shows that the resistance to Pharaoh does not start with Moses but actually begins with Shiphrah and Puah. It is their names that are shared and not the name of the king, highlighting these women as the heroes of this story. Gafney notes that Shiphrah and Puah are "the first deliverers in the book of deliverance."[15] Similarly, Frymer-Kensky comments that the midwives are among many women in Exodus who "become the saviors of early Israel and bring on the redemption from Egypt."[16] Exum points out that "this increasing concentration on women invites us to consider the significance of the fact that ancient Israelite storytellers gave women a crucial role in the initial stages of the major event in the nation's history."[17] The importance of Shiphrah and Puah is also emphasized by the structure of the passage, as their exchange with Pharaoh (vv. 15–21) is centered between the king's two messages to "his people" (vv. 8–14 and v. 22).[18] The storyteller makes it abundantly clear, by both content and structure, that it is these two women who frustrate the perlocutionary acts of the Egyptian king. Using Brueggemann's paradigm, it is these women who depict the "testimony" that counters Pharaoh's oppressive imagination.

The midwives' actions also invite intertextual conversations regarding other instances in Scripture in which women in similar situations using their words to cast a world that protects those who are vulnerable from men in power. For example, when directed by the king of Jericho to hand over the Israelite spies who had come to her house (Josh. 2:3), Rahab disobeys the king's order and hides the men instead (v. 4a). She then issues a series of assertives that start by agreeing with the world as it is described by the king (v. 4b) and then portrays the situation in a way that shields both herself (v. 4c) and the men (v. 5a; see table 4.4). Rahab ends her speech by directing the king to pursue the men in their supposed flight and assures him that he can overtake them (v. 5b). The performative structure of Rahab's response also counteracts the structure of the king's speech acts: whereas the king starts with a directive that incorporates an assertive and then issues another assertive, Rahab issues assertives and then ends with a directive that incorporates an assertive. Like the midwives, Rahab's assertives create an imaginary world that participates in the description of the world as it is portrayed by the oppressor's speech but deviates from it so that both herself and those in her care are protected from the king.

Another example is found in the story of David's escape from Saul with the help of his wife Michal (1 Sam. 19:9–17). After letting David down through a window (v. 12; cf. Rahab's similar action with the spies in Josh. 2:15), Michal fabricates a dummy clothed in David's attire that initially tricks Saul and his messengers into thinking that David is sick in bed (vv.

Table 4.4

Speaker	Speech		Speech Act
the king of Jericho (v. 3b)	הוֹצִיאִי הָאֲנָשִׁים הַבָּאִים אֵלַיִךְ אֲשֶׁר־בָּאוּ לְבֵיתֵךְ	"Bring out the men who came to you, who came to your house,"	Directive + Assertive 1
	כִּי לַחְפֹּר אֶת־כָּל־הָאָרֶץ בָּאוּ׃	"for they came to spy out the whole land."	Assertive 2
Rahab (v. 4b–5)	כֵּן בָּאוּ אֵלַי הָאֲנָשִׁים	"Correct, the men came to me,	Assertive 1
	וְלֹא יָדַעְתִּי מֵאַיִן הֵמָּה	"but I did not know where they were from.	Assertive 2
	וַיְהִי הַשַּׁעַר לִסְגּוֹר בַּחֹשֶׁךְ וְהָאֲנָשִׁים יָצָאוּ	And when it was time to close the gate at dark, the men went out;	Assertive 3
	לֹא יָדַעְתִּי אָנָה הָלְכוּ הָאֲנָשִׁים	I do not know where the men went.	Assertive 4
	רִדְפוּ מַהֵר אַחֲרֵיהֶם כִּי תַשִּׂיגוּם	Chase after them quickly, for you can overtake them!"	Directive + Assertive 5

12–14). When Saul directs for the bed to be brought to him so that he can kill David and the trick is discovered, he asks Michal why she has deceived him and allowed his enemy to escape (v. 17). Michal responds by saying, "He said to me, 'Let me go; why should I kill you?'" This (alleged) directive within Michal's assertive exonerates Michal by reinforcing Saul's view of David as a dangerous enemy. Indeed, Michal portrays herself as a passive figure in David's flight and even a victim, as opposed to the mastermind of his escape.

Other stories appear to play on the pattern that is on display in these stories but ultimately deviate from it. When Sisera, the army commander of King Jabin of Canaan, flees from battle and seeks refuge from Jael, he directs her to protect him by telling any pursuers that he is not there (see Judg. 4:17–20). He tells her, "Stand at the entrance of the tent, and if a man comes and asks you and says, 'Is a man here?' say, 'No'" (v. 20). Notably, Sisera attempts to micromanage and mansplain his own deliverance by Jael. Instead of following Sisera's directive, Jael takes matters into her own hands and kills her enemy Sisera in his sleep (vv. 21–22).

One shared feature in all of the stories mentioned here is that the oppressors all expect the women to act out of loyalty to them. In every case (except for Jael, who does not speak after Sisera's final directives), this assumption is reinforced and then exploited by the women's verbal responses. They perform assertives that affirm a part of the oppressor's perspective of the world and then add utterances that advance the success of their own perlocutionary acts.

Finally, the story of Shiphrah and Puah illustrates the practical nature of what it means to "fear (ירא) God," a prevalent theme that appears throughout Scripture. This description of the motivation for the midwives' actions is mentioned twice, first directly before their act of disobedience (v. 17) and then again when the storyteller emphasizes why God rewards them (v. 21). As Tremper Longman III points out, "The 'fear' of the 'fear of the Lord' is the sense of standing before the God who created everything, including humans whose very continued existence depends on him."[19] In such a context, "fear of God becomes synonymous with reverence, worship, and obedience to God's command."[20] For example, when Abraham passes God's test in the book of Genesis, the angel of Yhwh tells him, "Now I know that you fear God; you have not withheld your son, your only son, from me" (Gen. 22:12). While Abraham's situation involves a specific directive from God, the phrase is also used to reference moral behavior in light of a general desire to please God, such as when Abraham explains that he had deceived King Abimelech "because I thought, 'There is no fear of God in this place, and they will kill me on account of my wife'" (Gen. 20:11). To fear God is to refuse to harm others, as seen in the way that Job is described as someone who fears God and turns away from רע, a word often translated as "evil" that denotes a range of bad actions and situations (see Job 1:1).[21] When the midwives refuse to follow Pharaoh's immoral directive, they do so out of a conviction that God's authority surpasses that of Pharaoh. Just as Pharaoh can be viewed on the storyteller level as a paradigm for totalism, the midwives are portrayed as a paradigm for what it means to fear God.

The respective motivations for the actions of Pharaoh and the midwives offer a striking contrast between two concepts that elsewhere work together in Scripture, wisdom and the fear of God.[22] In the book of Proverbs, the fear of Yhwh is described as the beginning of knowledge, with fools despising wisdom (חכם) and instruction (see Prov. 1:7). Yet in this story, Pharaoh's efforts to quell the numbers of the Israelite people are done out of the desire to "act wisely" (חכם, v. 10) whereas the midwives' actions are due to their fear of God (vv. 17, 21). On the storyteller level, this opens up conversations involving different approaches to decision-making, prioritizing living to please God over against following the wisdom of scheming human leaders.[23]

CONCLUSIONS

Within the world of the narrative, Pharaoh and the midwives perform assertives that cast their world in ways that attempt to achieve their respective (and opposing) goals. Ironically, these worlds overlap, as the midwives resist

Pharaoh's aim by appealing to an aspect of the world that is cast by Pharaoh's toxic imagination.

Pharaoh's initial attempt to reduce the number and power of the Israelites utilizes assertives that portray them as a threat that the Egyptians must preemptively subdue and exploit. When his primary perlocutionary act fails, Pharaoh tries again. He uses assertives a bit differently in his attempt with the midwives, attaching directives to the situations that the midwives will actually face: if the child is a boy, then they should kill him. In both of his attempts, the success of Pharaoh's perlocutionary act depends upon his hearers viewing the world from the perspective of his toxic imagination.

When asked by the king to give the reason for why they did not follow his directives, Shiphrah and Puah assert that they actually face a situation that renders the options Pharaoh had offered them as obsolete. The motivation for the midwives' defiance of Pharaoh's directives, that they fear God, is known on the story level only to these brave women and to God. They claim to be unable to impact the situation entirely because of the (alleged) primitive and unsophisticated nature of the Hebrew women and how they differ from Egyptians. In this way, the midwives utilize the "othering" aspect of the imaginary world that Pharaoh had previously created with his words to the Egyptians in regard to the Israelites. Finally, Pharaoh tries a third time and bypasses the midwives, issuing his murderous directive straight to the people. It remains to be seen if he will finally succeed.

On the storyteller level, the narrative is told in ways that invite intertextual conversations surrounding the ongoing struggle between Pharaoh and the Israelites. In light of the covenant language found in Genesis, the king's fixation on the increasing number of Abraham's descendants and repeated attempts to quell it can be construed as an affront to God's plans that will inevitably lead to a clash between Pharaoh and Yhwh. As a prequel to the birth of Moses, this narrative reveals that Pharaoh was trying to prevent the birth of the leader that God will use to liberate them from Egypt and bestow upon them Yhwh's Torah. As a depiction of the inevitable and ongoing clash between those with Pharaoh's imagination and those who fear God, this narrative introduces a theme that runs throughout Scripture and transcends it, exposing such aspects of the audience's own world.

By portraying the midwives as heroic figures, this story invites audiences to reflect upon the courage of Shiphrah and Puah and the divine endorsement of their actions. These midwives provide a practical model of what it means to "fear" God in the context of resisting oppressive schemes. This story reveals that you cannot serve both God and Pharaoh, and audiences are encouraged to reject the predatory imagination of Pharaoh in their own world as they remember Shiphrah and Puah.

NOTES

1. Jezebel, the infamous Israelite queen, is a notable exception to the pattern of women resisting royal oppression. At the same time, she also fits within the pattern of royal oppression in that Queen Jezebel "uses power and authority like any male monarch," perfectly embodying the destructive power of the throne. Wilda C. Gafney, *Womanist Midrash: A Reintroduction to the Women of the Torah and the Throne* (Louisville: Westminster John Knox Press, 2017), 250.

2. Commenting on the richness of the semantic range of "know" (יָדַע), Sarna points out, "In the biblical conception, knowledge is not essentially or even primarily rooted in the intellect and mental activity. Rather, it is more experiential and is embedded in the emotions, so that it may encompass such qualities as contact, intimacy, concern, relatedness, and mutuality. Conversely, not to know is synonymous with dissociation, indifference, alienation, and estrangement; it culminates in callous disregard for another's humanity." Nahum M. Sarna, *Exodus* (Philadelphia: Jewish Publication Society, 1991), 5.

3. According to BDB, הִנֵּה is a demonstrative particle that can be translated as "Lo! Behold!" It is used for pointing out persons, things, places, and actions. Francis Brown, Samuel Rolles Driver, and Charles Augustus Briggs, *Enhanced Brown-Driver-Briggs Hebrew and English Lexicon* (Oxford: Clarendon Press, 1977), 243. Some interpreters have argued that such translations run the risk of confusing this particle with an imperative verb and insist that it functions in a manner similar to the pronouns, "this" and "that." Louis Dorn, "'Lo' and 'behold'—Translating the Hebrew Word Hinney," *Biblical Translator* 52 (2001): 222–29 (224). At the same time, Dorn states that the interjection is "a marker to indicate that what follows is worthy of attention." Thus, the function of this particle is nevertheless similar to imperative verbs such as "Look" and "Behold," which are used here by many translations.

4. For two helpful discussions of the names and designation of the midwives, see Sarna, *Exodus*, 7, and Tikva Frymer-Kensky, *Reading the Women of the Bible* (New York: Schocken Books, 2002), 24–25.

5. In arguing for a literal translation, Sarna translates הָאָבְנָיִם as "birthstool" and says that this term is "literally 'two stones,' [which] probably refers to the two bricks on which women in labor crouched opposite the midwife during parturition." Sarna, *Exodus*, 7. Similarly, the NRSV and NASB have "birthstool," and the NIV uses "delivery stool." Swanson notes that "pair of testicles" is also a possible translation, along with "delivery stool." James Swanson, *Dictionary of Biblical Languages with Semantic Domains: Hebrew (Old Testament)* (Oak Harbor: Logos Research Systems, Inc., 1997).

6. Gafney, *Womanist Midrash*, 90.

7. Gafney, *Womanist Midrash*, 90.

8. Frymer-Kensky, *Reading the Women of the Bible*, 25.

9. Sarna, *Exodus*, 5.

10. Brueggemann, *The Prophetic Imagination*, 9.

11. Brueggemann's thesis is, "*The task of prophetic ministry is to nurture, nourish, and evoke a consciousness and perception alternative to the consciousness and*

perception of the dominant culture around us" [italics original]. Brueggemann, *The Prophetic Imagination*, 3.

12. Brueggemann, *The Prophetic Imagination*, 6–25.

13. Walter Brueggemann, "Testimony that Breaks the Silence of Totalism," *Interpretation* 70:3 (2016): 275–87 (276).

14. Brueggemann, *The Prophetic Imagination*, 45.

15. Gafney, *Womanist Midrash*, 91.

16. Frymer-Kensky, *Reading the Women of the Bible*, 24.

17. Cheryl J. Exum, "'You Shall Let Every Daughter Live': A Study of Exodus 1:82:10," *Semeia* 28 (1983): 63–82 (68).

18. For another helpful chiastic view of the structure of this story, see Exum, "You Shall Let Every Daughter Live," 71–72.

19. Tremper Longman III, *The Fear of the Lord Is Wisdom: A Theological Introduction to Wisdom in Israel* (Grand Rapids: Baker Academic, 2017), 12.

20. H.F. Fuhs, "יָרֵא," *Theological Dictionary of the Old Testament* (Grand Rapids: Eerdmans, 1990), 290–315 (298).

21. See C. Dohmen and D. Rick, "רעע," *Theological Dictionary of the Old Testament* (Grand Rapids: Eerdmans, 2004), 561–88.

22. For an excellent study in the positive relationship between these concepts, see Longman, *The Fear of the Lord Is Wisdom*.

23. Another example in Scripture of wisdom being used as a weapon against someone is found in the story of Amnon's crime against his sister Tamar in 2 Samuel 13. In that story, it is Jonadab, described as "a very wise man" (אִישׁ חָכָם מְאֹד) who instructs Amnon on how to entrap and rape his sister (2 Sam. 13:3–5).

Chapter 5

Imagining the Land

A Duel of Descriptions in Numbers 13–14

A critical moment in ancient Israel's relationship with Yhwh occurs in Numbers 13–14, when Israel must decide if they will trust Yhwh and enter the land that God had promised to give them. After spies are sent into the land on a reconnaissance mission, they return and offer conflicting reports that force the community to choose a side. In his commentary on the book of Numbers, Olson notes:

> [T]he spy story is one of the most elaborate narratives in the whole of Numbers. Its several scenes and dialogues are carefully constructed. Suspense, irony, and dramatic dialogue give the reader a sense of the heightened importance of this narrative moment.[1]

It is not surprising that this story has much to offer for an investigation of its speech acts. On the story level, assertives play a decisive role in the conflicting perlocutionary acts of the clashing reports offered by the two groups of spies. Similarly, assertives function prominently in Moses's intercession on behalf of the people, after their rejection of Yhwh's plans leads to an existential crisis in their relationship with God. On the storyteller level, this narrative participates in intertextual conversations regarding the land's role in Israel's covenant with Yhwh, as well as the prevalent depiction of Yhwh as someone who can both forgive and punish. It also functions as a didactic story that other passages utilize as an exemplar for how those in a relationship with Yhwh should not act.

STORY LEVEL

The passage opens with a divine directive from Yhwh to Moses. God instructs him to "send for yourself men to investigate the land of Canaan, which I am giving to the Israelites. Send one man each per ancestral tribe, each one a leader among them" (Num. 13:2). Yhwh's assertion describing the land as a gift is central both in structure and in function. By describing the land of Canaan as "[that] which I am giving to the Israelites," Yhwh provides a reason for the directive as well as an invitation for the Israelites to imagine that the land belongs to God and is under Yhwh's control. In this way, the divine utterance constitutes two perlocutionary acts: (1) Yhwh intends for Moses to send spies into the land, and (2) for the Israelites to imagine the land in a particular way that will facilitate their entrance into it. As the story continues, it becomes clear that the first perlocutionary act succeeds, but the second one fails.

After the narrator reports the ways in which Moses follows Yhwh's directive regarding the initiation and composition of the investigation team (vv. 3–16), Moses then issues directives to the group. After identifying two geographic regions for them to explore, Moses instructs them in regard to their investigation of the land by alternating between a directive involving the land (הָאָרֶץ) and a specific aspect to analyze (vv. 17–20; see table 5.1). Notably, Moses fails to include an assertive that matches Yhwh's earlier assertive guiding their imagination to view the land as something that is under Yhwh's control. Instead, he uses questions that direct their imaginations to only look for two extremes. In regard to the land, they are directed to see if it is either good or bad, or rich or poor (especially in reference to the presence or lack of trees). In regard to the inhabitants, Moses directs them to see if they are either strong or weak, or if they are few or many. The towns are expected to be either open encampments or heavily fortified. Thus, Moses replaces a focus on the land as Yhwh's possession with an obsession for determining between extremes. His final directive invites them to focus on their own strength as they bring back some of the fruit of the land.

After offering a description of their investigation of the land (vv. 21–24), the narrator shares that the group returns after forty days to give their report and to show the fruit they had procured (vv. 25–26). Their report, offered to Moses in the presence of all the Israelites, consists of a series of assertives along with one directive (see table 5.2). They first offer a brief description of the land as flowing with milk and honey, along with a directive to look at the fruit they have brought (v. 27). This is followed by a series of assertives that start with a general description of the strength of the people and the towns and then involve a specific reference to seeing "the descendants of Anak." This is followed by a description of the people groups who live in each of the

Table 5.1

Verse	Speech		Speech Act	Focus
v. 17b	עֲלוּ זֶה בַּנֶּגֶב וַעֲלִיתֶם אֶת־הָהָר׃	Go up here into the Negev, and then go up into the hill country.	Directives	Geography
v. 18a	וּרְאִיתֶם אֶת־הָאָרֶץ מַה־הִוא	See the land: what is it like?	Directives	The land
v. 18b	וְאֶת־הָעָם הַיֹּשֵׁב עָלֶיהָ הֶחָזָק הוּא הֲרָפֶה הַמְעַט הוּא אִם־רָב׃	And the people who are living in it: are they strong? Are they weak? Are they few or are they many?	Directives	The people
v. 19a	וּמָה הָאָרֶץ אֲשֶׁר־הוּא יֹשֵׁב בָּהּ הֲטוֹבָה הִוא אִם־רָעָה	And what is the land like in which they are living? Is it good or bad?	Directives	The land
v. 19b	וּמָה הֶעָרִים אֲשֶׁר־הוּא יוֹשֵׁב בָּהֵנָּה הַבְּמַחֲנִים אִם בְּמִבְצָרִים׃	And what about the towns that they're living in, in open encampments or in fortifications?	Directives	The towns
v. 20a	וּמָה הָאָרֶץ הַשְּׁמֵנָה הִוא אִם־רָזָה הֲיֵשׁ־בָּהּ עֵץ אִם־אַיִן	And what about the land? Is it rich or poor? Are there trees in it or are there no trees?	Directives	The land
v. 20ba	וְהִתְחַזַּקְתֶּם וּלְקַחְתֶּם מִפְּרִי הָאָרֶץ	And you are to show your strength, and bring some of the fruit of the land.	Directives	General & specific charge

four regions. While the only clear directive in this report occurs in the beginning and involves looking at the fruit they brought, the assertives invite the Israelites to focus on the legendary strength of the people, the strength and size of the towns, and the way in which all of the land is already occupied. As a perlocutionary act, the report appears to be an attempt to dissuade the Israelites from entering the land by directing them to view it in a way that makes such a feat impossible.

The narrator does not directly share the Israelites' response to the report but implies that it involves unrest by saying that Caleb quieted the crowd (v. 30a). Tensions are high, and it is likely that there are differing opinions among those in the group on how to proceed. In an effort to persuade those in the group who are fearful of entering the land, Caleb performs a brief

Table 5.2

Verse	Speech		Speech Act	Focus
v. 27ab	בָּאנוּ אֶל־הָאָרֶץ אֲשֶׁר שְׁלַחְתָּנוּ	We came to the land to which you sent us;	Assertive	The spies
v. 27ba	וְגַם זָבַת חָלָב וּדְבַשׁ הִוא	also, it is flowing with milk and honey	Assertive	The land
v. 27bb	וְזֶה־פִּרְיָהּ׃	and this is its fruit.	Directive	The fruit
v. 28aa	אֶפֶס כִּי־עַז הָעָם הַיֹּשֵׁב בָּאָרֶץ	However, the people who are living in the land are strong	Assertive	The people
v. 28ab	וְהֶעָרִים בְּצֻרוֹת גְּדֹלֹת מְאֹד	And the towns are fortified, very large.	Assertive	The towns
vv. 28b–29	וְגַם־יְלִדֵי הָעֲנָק רָאִינוּ שָׁם׃ עֲמָלֵק יוֹשֵׁב בְּאֶרֶץ הַנֶּגֶב וְהַחִתִּי וְהַיְבוּסִי וְהָאֱמֹרִי יוֹשֵׁב בָּהָר וְהַכְּנַעֲנִי יֹשֵׁב עַל־הַיָּם וְעַל יַד הַיַּרְדֵּן׃	And also, we saw the descendants of Anak there. The Amalekites are living in the land of the Negeb, the Hittites, the Jebusites, and the Amorites are living in the hill country, and the Canaanites are living by the sea and along the Jordan.	Assertives	The people

directive that is supported with an assertive: "Let us go up at once and occupy it, for we are definitely able to prevail against it" (v. 30b). Wenham describes this utterance as an attempt to "rekindle their faith in the promises," noting that *"go up, occupy . . .* are key words in Exod. 3:8, 17; 33:3 and Lev. 20:24."[2] The other scouts counter Caleb's directive by performing an assertive that contradicts his assertive depicting the strength of the Israelites: "We are not able to go up against the people, for they are stronger than us" (v. 31). After the narrator steps in to emphasize that their report is an unfavorable one (v. 32a), the men go on to refute their initial description of the land. Whereas their first report had opened by describing the land as flowing with milk and honey, the men now describe it as "a land that devours those living in it" (v. 32b). They proceed to emphasize the legendary size and strength of the inhabitants by claiming that they saw the Nephilim there (v. 33), a reference to mythological giants and demigods (cf. Gen. 6:1–4). After the narrator offers an aside that offers an explanation for this ancient reference, the men offer a final assertive describing themselves as grasshoppers when compared to the inhabitants of the land. Pressler notes that "the scouts' report shifts from a realistic, albeit negatively slanted, description of the land to exaggerated, even nightmarish, language."[3] If it was not evident that the spies' first report had served as a perlocutionary act to dissuade the Israelites from entering the land, the revised report that counters Caleb's directive makes this intention clear.

The revised report achieves its purpose and perhaps more than the spies had intended. Not only do the Israelites refuse to enter the land, they also decide to return to Egypt. They begin by uttering expressives by lifting up their voices loudly and wailing (Num. 14:1), and move on to muttering against Moses and Aaron (v. 2). Their mutterings consist of expressives, assertives, and directives that imagine the past, present, and future in a bleak way that culminates in a directive for the group to consider going back to Egypt (see table 5.3). The narrator then interrupts their speech acts with a speech formula (4a) that introduces their directive/commissive for one another to choose a leader and go back to Egypt (v. 4b). While previous traditions include Israel murmuring against Yhwh (e.g., Num. 11:20), George Coats points out that "here, for the first time, the murmuring is followed by a move to return to Egypt."[4] He goes on to note that this murmuring "involves not simply an expression of a wish that the Exodus had not occurred or a challenge of Moses' authority in executing the Exodus, but now an overt move to reverse the Exodus."[5] Indeed, expressives have led to directives. As Pressler notes, such an act of returning to Egypt "represents a *total* rejection of their relationship to the God who had delivered them from Egypt and adopted them."[6] By adopting the spies' perspective of the land and their own inferiority, the assembly of Israelites now views their past

Table 5.3

Ch. 14	Speech		Speech Act
v. 2bb	לוּ־מַתְנוּ בְּאֶרֶץ מִצְרַיִם אוֹ בַּמִּדְבָּר הַזֶּה לוּ־מָתְנוּ:	"If only we had died in the land of Egypt! Or, in this wilderness if only we had died!"	Expressives / Assertives (past)
v. 3a	וְלָמָה יהוה מֵבִיא אֹתָנוּ אֶל־הָאָרֶץ הַזֹּאת לִנְפֹּל בַּחֶרֶב	"Why is Yhwh bringing us into this land to fall by the sword?"	Directive / Assertive (present)
v. 3b	נָשֵׁינוּ וְטַפֵּנוּ יִהְיוּ לָבַז	"Our women and our little ones will become plunder!"	Assertive (future)
v. 3c	הֲלוֹא טוֹב לָנוּ שׁוּב מִצְרָיְמָה:	"Would it not be good for us to go back to Egypt?"	Directive
v. 4b	נִתְּנָה רֹאשׁ וְנָשׁוּבָה מִצְרָיְמָה:	"Let us choose a leader and let us return to Egypt!"	Directives / Commissives

rescue from Egypt in a negative light and decides to attempt to revert back to their original situation. Yhwh's response will be equally absolute in its scope.

Israel's two leaders respond by falling on their faces, a sign of lament. Wenham points out that in the book of Numbers such an act "usually anticipates some great act of judgment (cf. 16:4, 22, 45; 20:6)."[7] Joshua and Caleb are described as tearing their clothes, a more conventional gesture of distress.[8] They attempt to change the assembly's mind by performing their own series of assertives and directives (see table 5.4). They open with three assertives concerning the land, with the first and third offering a positive description of the land (vv. 7b, 8b) and the middle assertive displaying the possibility of Yhwh giving them the land (v. 8a). They then perform three directives and three assertives. A general directive opposing the act of rebelling against Yhwh (v. 9a) is followed by a chiastic ordering that positions the three assertives that describe the people of the land and the Israelites (v. 9bb, 9ca, 9cb) within two directives for them not to fear the land's inhabitants (vv. 9ba, 9cc). The chiastic structuring of these assertives constitutes an impressive attempt to refocus the Israelites' imagination away from the fearmongering

Table 5.4

Verse	Speech		Speech Act	Focus
v. 7b	הָאָרֶץ אֲשֶׁר עָבַרְנוּ בָהּ לָתוּר אֹתָהּ טוֹבָה הָאָרֶץ מְאֹד מְאֹד:	"The land that we passed through to investigate, it is a very, very good land."	Assertive	The land
v. 8a	אִם־חָפֵץ בָּנוּ יהוה וְהֵבִיא אֹתָנוּ אֶל־הָאָרֶץ הַזֹּאת וּנְתָנָהּ לָנוּ	"If Yhwh delights in us, he will bring us into this land and give it to us,"	Assertive	Yhwh, the Israelites, & the land
v. 8b	אֶרֶץ אֲשֶׁר־הִוא זָבַת חָלָב וּדְבָשׁ:	"a land that is flowing with milk and honey."	Assertive	The land
v. 9a	אַךְ בַּיהוה אַל־תִּמְרֹדוּ	"Only, do not to rebel against Yhwh."	Directive	The Israelites & Yhwh
v. 9ba	וְאַתֶּם אַל־תִּירְאוּ אֶת־עַם הָאָרֶץ	"And you, do not fear the people of the land,"	Directive	The Israelites & the people of the land
v. 9bb	כִּי לַחְמֵנוּ הֵם	"for they are our bread."	Assertive	The people of the land
v. 9ca	סָר צִלָּם מֵעֲלֵיהֶם	"Their shade has turned from over them,	Assertive	The people of the land
v. 9cb	וַיהוה אִתָּנוּ	and Yhwh is with us."	Assertive	Yhwh
v. 9cc	אַל־תִּירָאֻם:	"Do not fear them."	Directive	The Israelites

imaginations of the other spies and toward viewing the land as a good gift from God that is not threatened by the land's inhabitants.

Joshua and Caleb's perlocutionary act fails, evidenced by the assembly's reported threat to stone them (v. 10a). The narrator introduces Yhwh's response by sharing that Yhwh's glory appears in the tent of meeting, before all of the Israelites (v. 10b). Many interpreters have noticed that the ensuing conversation between Yhwh and Moses holds many similarities to the exchange they had in response to the earlier infamous event involving the golden calf (Exod. 32).[9] As in their exchange regarding the golden calf, Yhwh begins by directing Moses's attention to the faithlessness of the people and then performs a commissive indicating that God plans to eradicate them and then make Moses into a great nation (Num. 14:11–12; cf. Exod. 32:7–10). As before, Moses intercedes for the people by casting an imagined world that would result from such a divine response to be an undesirable outcome in regard to Yhwh's reputation (vv. 13–16, cf. the discussion of Exod. 32:11–13 in chapter 3). Whereas previously Moses had created this imagined world by using directives, this time he uses assertives. In both cases, Moses performs a final assertive that would (allegedly) be uttered by others concerning Yhwh: in Exodus 32:12, Moses says that the Egyptians would say that Yhwh brought them out of Egypt in order to kill them, whereas in Numbers 14:16, the nations would say that Yhwh was not able to bring this people into the land that had been divinely promised to them.

After creating the imaginary world with his assertives as a foundation, Moses proceeds to perform the directive portion of his intercession. Moses directs God to act in accordance with something that Yhwh had spoken earlier (v. 17). According to Moses, Yhwh had self-identified as someone who is "slow to anger, and abounding in commitment, forgiving iniquity and transgression, yet certainly not leaving the guilty unpunished, attending to the sin of parents upon the children, to the third and the fourth generation" (v. 18). He then issues his final directive, that God "please pardon the iniquity of this people, according to the greatness of your commitment, just as you have forgiven this people, from Egypt as far as here." Overall, the perlocutionary act of persuading Yhwh to forgive the Israelites functions by projecting the world in an unfavorable way if God proceeds with the previous divine plan, and then directing God to act in a different way that nevertheless fits with God's previous words and actions.

Moses's perlocutionary act is successful, as God quickly acquiesces to the directive to forgive the Israelites by saying, "I forgive, according to your words" (v. 20). At the same time, Yhwh continues in a response that fits with the complicated nature of the previous testimony referenced by Moses. God delivers two judgment speeches that consist of assertives and commissives regarding the forthcoming divine actions and their consequences (vv. 21–25

& 26–35). In both judgment speeches, Yhwh includes the oath formula, "as I live" (v. 21, 28), an addition that enhances the direction of fit that allows these assertives and commissives to reach the level found in declaratives. By performing these utterances with this oath formula, Yhwh ensures that these acts will come about.

God references the land (הָאָרֶץ) three times in each judgment speech. In the first speech, the first two references are used in assertives: that all the land will be filled with the glory of Yhwh (v. 21) and that none of the people who saw Yhwh's glory and yet disobeyed God shall see the land (v. 23). The third reference is used in a commissive, that Yhwh will bring Caleb into the land to be possessed by his descendants because he followed God (v. 24). Yhwh opens the second judgment speech by directing the focus back to the Israelites' previous complaints and commits to doing what they had said earlier (v. 28). Notably, in the first land reference in this speech, God grants the Israelites' expressive involving their preference to have died in the wilderness (see v. 2); none of them will enter the land except for Caleb and Joshua (vv. 29–30). Unlike typical expressives, the one uttered by the Israelites will ironically now fit with the narrative world. The second reference to the land involves a commissive indicating that Yhwh will bring their children into the land but without matching their previous description of the children becoming plunder (v. 31). The third land reference explicitly connects the time period that their children will wander in the wilderness to the time that the spies were in the land (v. 34).

This time, Moses does not attempt to intercede for the Israelites. The passage closes with the narrator describing the deaths of all the spies except for Joshua and Caleb (vv. 36–38), and then a brief narrative in which the Israelites attempt (and fail) to enter the promised land on their own power (vv. 39–45).

Storyteller Level

This narrative participates in numerous intertextual conversations, including a thematic one involving the land as a major factor in Israel's relationship with Yhwh. It also provides a powerful narrative illustration of a dominant portrayal of the Old Testament's testimony about Yhwh as someone who is great in commitment (חֶסֶד) while also being someone who can bring punishment.[10] This may be a reason for why other passages utilize this story as an exemplar in attempts to dissuade their own audiences from rejecting Yhwh (see below).

Whereas the story level displays the persuasive power of competing depictions of the land, the storyteller level presents the land as a dominant theme in Scripture's portrayal of Israel's relationship with Yhwh. Brueggemann has offered a compelling argument that "land is a central, if not *the central theme of biblical faith*."[11] He notes that "Israel's faith is essentially a journeying in and out of land," and suggests that "its faith can be organized around these focuses."[12] Brueggemann states:

> The land for which Israel yearns and which it remembers is never unclaimed space but is always *a place with Yahweh,* a place well filled with memories of life with him and promise from him and vows to him. It is land that provides the central assurance to Israel of its historicality, that it will be and always must be concerned with actual rootage in a place which is a repository for commitment and therefore identity.[13]

Indeed, God's covenant with Abraham and Sarah, that their descendants will become a blessing to all the nations and families of the earth, is directly connected to the land of Canaan (e.g., Gen. 12:1–7). After Yhwh rescues the Israelites from the land of Egypt, this land is the strategic location where Israel will follow Yhwh's Torah as a way to bear witness to the nations (e.g., Deut. 4:5–8). Moses also warns the Israelites that if they reject Yhwh, then they will lose the land (e.g., Deut. 4:25–27). Throughout Israel's story, the land is always a central player in their identity as God's people. This particular story in Numbers 13–14 explicitly connects Israel's ability to live in the land with their willingness to trust in God's strength instead of their own, a key theological message in the intertextual conversations involving land in Scripture.

When starting from the perspective of the audience, the storyteller level includes a fascinating similarity to the tension on the story level in regard to whether or not Israel should occupy the land of Canaan. While many interpreters agree that Israel should enter the land, others find themselves siding with the Canaanites as they point to elements in the story that are associated with colonialism. For example, after pointing to the way in which postcolonial readings of the Bible will "expose and protest against the bible's place among colonial literature," Havea states:

> [A] postcolonial reading of the book of Numbers will thus protest the way it constructs and narrates Israel in the wilderness in such a way that the account also numbs any interest in the land and the people of the land in the wilderness.[14]

Havea goes on to declare, "With regard to the book of Numbers, I favor the native peoples of Moab, Edom, Amalek, Midian, and their wilderness neighbors, over and against the people and cause of Israel. Israel, as Balak rightly complained, was trespassing (Num. 22–24)."[15] There is no doubt that the biblical passages that speak of Israel's conquest of the land of Canaan have been used to justify various acts of colonization worldwide. At the same time, there is a strong case to be made that these applications are inappropriate. For example, Marc Brett points out:

> In the history of colonization, it is clear that generations of Europeans became intoxicated with their ideas of racial superiority and civilization, and the Bible was caught up in the destructive consequences. Biblical texts were often used as colonial instruments of power, exploited with pre-emptive and self-interested strategies of reading.[16]

Brett goes on to state that despite this application, "most biblical texts were produced by authors who were themselves subject to the shifting tides of ancient empires."[17] Goldingay points to the importance of inquiring into the text's own purposes for telling the stories about Israel's conquest of the land:

> So why did First Testament Israel tell a story about its ancestors' speedy conquest of the land under Joshua? The past and present application of the text presupposes that Israel's acts are precedents for similar acts on the readers' part. But there is no indication in the text that this is so—any more than is the case with an act such as Abraham's offering of Isaac. The point about the stories is not to provide warrant for human action but to testify to divine action. They indicate that Yhwh gave Israel the land.[18]

While conversations surrounding the misuse of the Bible and tensions within the Old Testament's portrayal of Israel's possession of the land are important and can lead to fruitful insights, it is also important to explore the perlocutionary intent of the storytellers.

This passage highlights and illustrates a prominent testimony in Scripture concerning Yhwh's character. A chiastic structuring of this passage highlights Moses's intercession as a key aspect of the entire episode (see table 5.5). The story begins and ends with the identity of the men who spy out the land (A) and their fate (A'). The next level into the chiasm draws on 40 as a significant number, first for the number of days the spies were in the land and their reports (B), corresponding to the way in which the length of Israel's punishment for their response to the reports is patterned after this number (B'). The third level involves the people's complaints, including their expressives, assertives, and commissives/directives to return to Egypt (C). Consequently, Yhwh references their complaining and issues commissives to bring about their expressives and assertives, due to their directive (C'). Caleb's attempt to change the people's minds (D) and Yhwh's corresponding response to Caleb (D') provide the last level surrounding the center of the chiasm, Moses's intercession (E). This interpretation of the structure of the passage suggests that one of the purposes of this narrative is to emphasize Moses's act of intercession.

Table 5.5

A—Divine directive to send <u>men to spy out the land</u>; assertives describing the men that are sent (Joshua's name emphasized); Moses's directives to the men; assertives describing their spying of the land;	vv. 1–24
B—Spies return after <u>40 Days</u>; reports (spies→ Caleb → spies);	vv. 25–33
C—People <u>complain</u> and perform expressives and assertives; directive to go back to Egypt;	vv. 1–4
D—<u>Caleb</u> attempts again, fails;	vv. 5–10a
E—Yhwh's reaction, Moses's intercession, and Yhwh's response;	vv. 10b–23
D'—Yhwh's commissive regarding bringing <u>Caleb</u> into the land, directive for Israel to set out for the wilderness;	vv. 24–25
C'—Yhwh references Israel <u>complaining</u>, and performs commissives that God will do as they said in their expressives and assertives because of their directive;	vv. 26–32
B'—Consequences involve <u>40 years, due to the spies' 40 days;</u>	vv. 33–35
A'—Assertives describing the divinely appointed death of the <u>men who spied out the land</u> (with the exception of Caleb and Joshua).	vv. 36–38

This central placement of Moses's intercession within the narrative draws attention to the assertives that he uses to persuade Yhwh. The first group of assertives focuses on Yhwh's reputation among the inhabitants of the land (vv. 13–14a), specifically regarding God's presence in the midst of the Israelites (v. 14b) and what will be said if Yhwh destroys the Israelites (vv. 15–16). The second part of Moses's intercession includes a reference to Yhwh's own previous self-description (v. 18), which is centered between two directives for Yhwh to act in accordance with these words (vv. 17, 19–20). Appealing to the world previously created by God's own words, Moses describes Yhwh as "slow to anger, and abounding in commitment, forgiving iniquity and transgression, yet certainly not leaving the guilty unpunished, attending to the sin of parents upon the children, to the third and the fourth generation" (v. 18; cf. Exod. 20:5; Exod. 34:6–7). This assertive is viewed by many interpreters to be the central affirmation in Scripture of Israel's understanding of their God. For example, Brueggemann uses this confession in Exodus 34:6–7 to organize his magisterial overview of Israel's understanding of God that holds the inherent tension between Yhwh as someone who both forgives and who brings punishment.[19] This narrative provides a memorable illustration of both of these main qualities simultaneously. While the characteristic of being "slow to anger" might not entirely fit in this instance, Yhwh's abounding commitment is on full display when God forgives the community and continues in the relationship.[20] At the same time, the guilty in this story experience punishment for their sin, and the consequence of wandering in the wilderness impacts their children.

While a chiasm draws attention to Moses's successful intercession, another chiasm within the larger one highlights the punishment. This one incorporates Yhwh's five references to the wilderness in the final judgment speech; the wilderness (and not the land) will be the location where the sinful generation will die, and the chiasm highlights the situation that Israel's children will endure during this time of punishment (see table 5.6).

This chiasm might function as an attempt to change the focus of the Israelites away from the land and toward the wilderness. (Based on Israel's ensuing actions in vv. 39–45, this perlocutionary act fails.) On the storyteller level, interpreters are similarly invited to turn their attention to the wilderness. Brueggemann offers some helpful insights into this theme:

> Wilderness is not the place of destiny Israel or anyone else would prefer. But Israel is a people created in impossibility (Sarah) and sustained against every deathly prognosis. Israel lives only by miracle. It never decides its destiny is landlessness, but it concludes in these traditions that landlessness as a way to land is a bearable, even celebrative event because Yahweh is there with his people. And because Yahweh is there, gifts are given, healings emerge, newness governs, and nothing grows old. It is against all the wise expectations of this age, of all those who would reasonably leave Israel there to die.[21]

Even though wilderness is a landless liminal space that holds the threat of death, it can be a place of growth and even security if Yhwh is involved.

Another conversation on the storyteller level involves a recognition of the ways in which other biblical passages use this story as a teachable moment of what *not* to do, an exemplar that must never be repeated. For example, Goldingay notes that "Psalm 78 systematically portrays the wilderness journey as a period of ongoing rebellion from which the subsequent community needs to learn."[22] He points to the way that verse 8 teaches the audience that "they should not be like their ancestors, a refractory, rebellious generation, a generation that did not make its mind firm, whose spirit was not faithful to God."[23] Similarly, Psalm 95:8–11 draws on this story (as well as Exod. 17 and Num. 20) in issuing the following directive and assertives:

> Do not harden your hearts, like at Meribah, like on the day at Massah in the wilderness, when your ancestors tested me. They tried me, though they had seen my action; for forty years I loathed the generation and said, "They are a people whose hearts go astray, they have not acknowledged my ways," of whom I swore in my anger, "if they come into my rest."

Table 5.6

"In this wilderness your corpses will fall."	v. 29a
"And you, your corpses shall fall *in this wilderness*	v. 32
and your children shall be shepherding *in the wilderness* for forty years, and shall bear your faithlessness	v. 33a–b
until your corpses come to an end *in the wilderness.*"	v. 33c
" . . . I, Yhwh, have spoken. If I don't surely do this to this entire bad assembly gathered together against me; *in this wilderness* they will come to an end, there they shall die."	v. 35

While God might have quickly been able to forgive the Israelites on the story level after Moses's intercession, it is evident that God does not forget on the storyteller level.

CONCLUSIONS

In a pivotal moment after their exodus from Egypt, Israel must choose how to proceed after the spies who had been sent by Moses present clashing descriptions of the land. The competing ways of imagining the land correspond with two ways of viewing their relationship with Yhwh; they will either trust their God and enter the land, or they will reject Yhwh. The current study has pointed out the persuasive power of assertives in this story, beginning with the way in which Moses directs the spies to look for extremes in the land rather than viewing it to be under Yhwh's control. While it is not clear that Moses intended to shift their focus away from Yhwh's connection with the land and toward the strength of the inhabitants, the majority report from the spies demonstrates such an effect. After the Israelites adopt the negative perspective and make plans to return to Egypt, Yhwh responds to their denial by rejecting them and commits to starting over with Moses. The power of assertives is again on display as Moses intercedes for the people by referencing Yhwh's own previous assertives describing God's character. Persuaded, Yhwh forgives the community but also pronounces a forty-year period of punishment in the wilderness. On the storyteller level, this narrative is told in ways that illuminate the importance of the land to Israel's relationship with Yhwh. It also highlights Moses's intercession, with the results providing a practical application of a dominant portrayal of Yhwh's characteristics that is utilized by other passages as a prime example of what might appropriately be called a "teachable moment."

NOTES

1. 'Dennis T. Olson, *Numbers* (Louisville: Westminster John Knox Press, 2012), 75.'

2. Gordon J. Wenham, *Numbers: An Introduction and Commentary* (Downers Grove: Inter-Varsity Press, 1981), 120.

3. Carolyn Pressler, *Numbers* (Nashville: Abingdon Press, 2017), 117.

4. George Coats, *Rebellion in the Wilderness: The Murmuring Motif in the Wilderness Traditions of the Old Testament* (Nashville: Abingdon Press, 1968), 146.

5. Coats, *Rebellion in the Wilderness*, 146.

6. Pressler, *Numbers*, 120.

7. Wenham, *Numbers*, 121.

8. Wenham, *Numbers,* 121.

9. Jacob Milgrom points out that these two stories are distinct in that they are the only instances where God threatens to destroy all the people and to start over in making a new nation out of Moses. Jacob Milgrom, *Numbers* (Philadelphia: The Jewish Publication Society, 1990), 99.

10. For a discussion of חֶסֶד, see chapter 7 of this book.

11. Walter Brueggemann, *The Land: Place as Gift, Promise, and Challenge in Biblical Faith* (Philadelphia: Fortress Press, 1977), 3 [italics original].

12. Brueggemann, *The Land,* 3, 14. Another insightful reflection on the significance of the land for Israel's understanding of themselves and their God is found in Bruce C. Birch, Walter Brueggemann, Terence E. Fretheim, and David L. Petersen, *A Theological Introduction to the Old Testament*, 2nd ed. (Nashville: Abingdon Press, 2011), 175–213.

13. Brueggemann, *The Land,* 5–6.

14. 'Jione Havea, "Numbing Numbers: Land and People of the Wilderness," in *Postcolonial Commentary and the Old Testament*, ed. Hemchand Gossai (London: T&T Clark, 2018), 57–69, 59.'

15. Havea, "Numbing Numbers," 59.

16. Mark G. Brett, *Decolonizing God: The Bible in the Tides of Empire* (Sheffield: Sheffield Phoenix Press, 2008), 31.

17. Brett, *Decolonizing God*, 31.

18. John Goldingay, *Old Testament Theology, Volume One: Israel's Gospel* (Downers Grove: InterVarsity Press, 2003), 491–92.

19. Walter Brueggemann, *Theology of the Old Testament: Testimony, Dispute, Advocacy* (Minneapolis: Fortress Press, 1997).

20. As Katharine Doob Sakenfeld says,

> The content of God's forgiveness here is the nondestruction of the *people,* the very continuation of God's relationship to the *community* as God's community. It is the *hesed*-based decision not to create a new nation of Moses or anyone else, and not to disinherit this community because of its unfaithfulness. (Katharine Doob Sakenfeld, *Numbers: Journeying with God* (Grand Rapids: Eerdmans, 1995), 90–91 [italics original].

21. Brueggemann, *The Land*, 44.

22. Goldingay, *Israel's Gospel*, 465–66.
23. Goldingay, *Israel's Gospel*, 466.

Chapter 6

Imagining the Temple in 2 Samuel 7:1–17

A key moment in the overarching narrative of Israel's relationship with Yhwh occurs when God makes an unconditional commitment to King David (2 Sam. 7:1–17). Often called the "David covenant" by interpreters, this commitment alone is worthy of the vast amount of attention that it has received. However, it is also helpful to explore the way in which this commitment appears in the origin story for the concept of building a temple for Yhwh. In fact, Yhwh commits to building a "house" (dynasty) for David after David proposes that he build a "house" (temple) for Yhwh. In 2 Samuel 7:1–17, the speech acts performed by David and Yhwh exhibit conflicting viewpoints concerning God's accessibility. David's utterances start from his own identity as king as he imagines that God should similarly reside in a house, a temple. The world that is created by David's imagination is one in which God's life mirrors that of the human king, who can do things for God. Yhwh performs utterances that expose limitations in such a view, especially in light of how God has previously lived and operated among the Israelites. God reverses the power dynamic involved in David's proposal; while Yhwh will allow a temple to be built eventually, God commits to building a permanent house for David. In this way, God's words create a world in which God is the ultimate authority and is someone who can do something for David. From an intertextual perspective, this passage contributes to conversations involving views of the tension involved in having a temple for God, as well as discussions on the autonomy and accessibility of God.

STORY LEVEL

The scene opens with an exchange of directives between King David and the prophet Nathan (vv. 1–3). The narrator sets the scene by sharing that the king has been living in his house while enjoying the safety that Yhwh has provided from all his enemies (v. 1). The narrator references David only as "the king" three times in this section, suggesting that he is speaking from his royal position of authority. Drawing attention to the difference in his own house when compared to Yhwh's living situation, the king notes that he is living in a "house of cedar" whereas the ark of God is living inside a tent (v. 2). Van Wijk-Bos notes that at this point it is "not clear that the king is asking for advice, since he merely makes an observation."[1] She goes on to say that "Nathan clearly takes the statement as a question and offers counsel."[2] Indeed, Nathan realizes that David's assertive is actually functioning as a directive and responds with a directive of his own, "Go, do all that is in your mind" (v. 3a). He then offers an assertive providing a reason that justifies this directive, that Yhwh is with him (v. 3b). This response signals that the king's directive has functioned as a perlocutionary act for the prophet to give him permission to act, presumably in a way that resolves the discrepancy between the two dwelling places. While the king's perlocutionary act is initially successful (Nathan grants him permission to do whatever is on his mind), that success is temporary as Yhwh will soon intervene.

While it is clear that David is attempting to gain permission to build a temple for Yhwh, interpreters have discussed different possibilities for what David might hope to achieve in such an endeavor. Some have suggested that David is simply doing something that would be expected of a king. As Mellish states, "It was a common practice in the ancient Near East that a king would build a temple in a city he conquered as a sign of respect and reverence to the god he worshipped. David was no different."[3] Brueggemann points out that David also would have practical and political reasons for such a proposal, as a temple would legitimize his regime. "The obvious answer to the problem of legitimacy characteristic of every ruler in the ancient world is to build a temple. Give God a permanent residence that will solidify the regime."[4] Wolpe suggests that David is trying to affect a "power balance" he has with God and says, "David has survived and is king. He is deeply indebted to God. To build a Temple would, in some sense, put God in his debt. It would change the relationship between them."[5] Interpreters tend to agree that building a temple for Yhwh would be beneficial for David, although they disagree on how exactly he would benefit.

While David might benefit from building Yhwh a house, it immediately becomes clear that Yhwh does not view it as beneficial for God. That night, God issues two directives for Nathan to deliver two groups of speech acts "to my servant, to David" (vv. 5a, 8a). A designation that stands in stark contrast to the narrator's use of "the king," Yhwh presents David as someone who is personally committed to serving Yhwh. Both groupings of speech acts work together in a divine attempt to first counter and then to transform David's imagination (what Nathan had described as all that the king "has in mind"). The first group alternates between directives and assertives, whereas the second group contains alternating asssertives and commissives. The first group attempts to draw David's focus away from the need for him to build a house for Yhwh, and the second group invites David to imagine a future world that will exist after Yhwh commits to building him a house.

Yhwh opens the first group of illocutionary acts with a directive ("Go and say to my servant, to David") that is followed by a speech formula ("Thus says Yhwh"). After this introduction, Nathan is to perform a directive that is followed by two assertives and then another directive (see table 6.1). The first directive asks if David is even supposed to build Yhwh a house in which to live (v. 5bb). The ensuing assertive presupposes a negative answer to this question by starting out with the word "because" (כִּי) and then the next assertive describes Yhwh's previous actions among the Israelites in a way that demonstrates why such a house is unnecessary. Rather than living in a house, Yhwh has been moving around with the people in a tent and tabernacle (v. 6). The second question asks if Yhwh, during this time, had ever asked any

Table 6.1

v. 5a	לֵךְ וְאָמַרְתָּ אֶל־עַבְדִּי אֶל־דָּוִד	Go and say to my servant, to David:	Directive
v. 5ba	כֹּה אָמַר יהוה	Thus says Yhwh:	Speech formula
v. 5bb	הַאַתָּה תִּבְנֶה־לִּי בַיִת לְשִׁבְתִּי׃	Are you to build me a house to live in?	Directive
v. 6	כִּי לֹא יָשַׁבְתִּי בְּבַיִת לְמִיּוֹם הַעֲלֹתִי אֶת־בְּנֵי יִשְׂרָאֵל מִמִּצְרַיִם וְעַד הַיּוֹם הַזֶּה וָאֶהְיֶה מִתְהַלֵּךְ בְּאֹהֶל וּבְמִשְׁכָּן׃	Because I have not lived in a house since the day that I brought up the Israelites from Egypt until this day; and I have been going about in a tent and in a tabernacle.	Assertives
v. 7	בְּכֹל אֲשֶׁר־הִתְהַלַּכְתִּי בְּכָל־בְּנֵי יִשְׂרָאֵל הֲדָבָר דִּבַּרְתִּי אֶת־אַחַד שִׁבְטֵי יִשְׂרָאֵל אֲשֶׁר צִוִּיתִי לִרְעוֹת אֶת־עַמִּי אֶת־יִשְׂרָאֵל לֵאמֹר לָמָּה לֹא־בְנִיתֶם לִי בֵּית אֲרָזִים׃	Everywhere I went about among all the Israelites, did I speak with one of the tribes of Israel whom I commanded to shepherd my people Israel, saying, "Why have you not built me a house of cedar?"	Directive

of the tribes of Israel why they had not built God such a house (v. 7). As with the first question, the implied answer to this inquiry is negative. As van Wijk-Bos notes, "A significant statement about the preference of Israel's God, who from the days of Israel's liberation on was not stationary, is surrounded by the questions of verses 5 and 7."[6] The placement of these significant assertives within the directives is designed to make David reflect upon them. In this way, the first group of illocutionary acts works together to suggest that a world in which building a temple for God is unnecessary and even inappropriate.

After countering David's idea of building Yhwh a temple, God directs Nathan to perform a second group of illocutionary acts that invite David to imagine what Yhwh will do for him (see table 6.2). The addition of "now thus" (וְעַתָּה כֹּה) in the opening directive ("Now thus you shall say to my servant, to David") signals the strategic ordering of these two worlds. The use of God's military name, "Yhwh of Armies," in the ensuing speech formula ("Thus says Yhwh of Armies") signals divine action. God then proceeds with assertives and commissives that create a world that exists in light of Yhwh's commitment to David, first as it pertains to David and all Israel (vv. 8b–11b) and then as it pertains to David's heir and future kingdom (vv. 11c–16). Whereas David had proposed building a house (בַּיִת) for Yhwh, God commits to building a house (בַּיִת) for David.

In the first portion of this grouping of illocutionary acts (vv. 8b–11b), Yhwh issues assertives and commissives that work together to cast a world in which David and Israel experience success and security. Yhwh begins with two assertives that describe David's previous rise to the throne and his current military success as the result of divine actions (vv. 8b–9a). The first assertive fits with aspects of the earlier narrative regarding David's rise, particularly in the tradition of Samuel anointing David (1 Sam. 16:1–13). Notably, Yhwh does not refer to David as a king here, but as a ruler. Millish suggests that this choice is significant:

> The term used here for *leader* (*nagid*) . . . is distinct from the term for "king" (*melek*). The term *nagid* emphasized the custodial role of the leader who presided over "God's people." Whereas a "king" represented a form of centralized control and power that was often abused and misused. The imagery and language of shepherding is also significant here because God's greatest leaders started out as shepherds before they took on leadership roles.[7]

The way in which Yhwh avoids calling David a king fits with the way God calls David "my servant" and then casts a world that emphasizes David's relationship with Yhwh rather than his royal position. The second assertive fits with the narrator's description of David's current secure situation that opens the story (cf. 2 Sam. 7:1). Yhwh has been with David everywhere

Table 6.2

v. 8a	וְעַתָּה כֹּה־תֹאמַר לְעַבְדִּי לְדָוִד	Now thus you shall say to my servant, to David:	Directive
v. 8ba	כֹּה אָמַר יְהוָה צְבָאוֹת	Thus says Yhwh of Armies	Speech formula
v. 8b	אֲנִי לְקַחְתִּיךָ מִן־הַנָּוֶה מֵאַחַר הַצֹּאן לִהְיוֹת נָגִיד עַל־עַמִּי עַל־יִשְׂרָאֵל:	I took you from the pasture, from following the flock, to be ruler over my people, over Israel.	Assertive
v. 9a	וָאֶהְיֶה עִמְּךָ בְּכֹל אֲשֶׁר הָלַכְתָּ וָאַכְרִתָה אֶת־כָּל־אֹיְבֶיךָ מִפָּנֶיךָ	And I have been with you everywhere you went, and I cut off all your enemies from before you.	Assertive
v. 9b	וְעָשִׂתִי לְךָ שֵׁם גָּדוֹל כְּשֵׁם הַגְּדֹלִים אֲשֶׁר בָּאָרֶץ:	And I will make for you a great name, like the name of the great ones who are in the land.	Commissive
v. 10a	וְשַׂמְתִּי מָקוֹם לְעַמִּי לְיִשְׂרָאֵל וּנְטַעְתִּיו	And I will appoint a place for my people, for Israel, and I will plant them.	Commissive
v. 10b–11a	וְשָׁכַן תַּחְתָּיו וְלֹא יִרְגַּז עוֹד וְלֹא־יֹסִיפוּ בְנֵי־עַוְלָה לְעַנּוֹתוֹ כַּאֲשֶׁר בָּרִאשׁוֹנָה: וּלְמִן־הַיּוֹם אֲשֶׁר צִוִּיתִי שֹׁפְטִים עַל־עַמִּי יִשְׂרָאֵל	They will dwell in their own place and no longer tremble; children of wickedness will no longer afflict them as they did previously, from the day I appointed judges over my people Israel.	Assertives
11b	וַהֲנִיחֹתִי לְךָ מִכָּל־אֹיְבֶיךָ	And I will give you rest from all of your enemies.	Commissive
11ca	וְהִגִּיד לְךָ יְהוָה	And Yhwh tells you	Speech formula
11cb	כִּי־בַיִת יַעֲשֶׂה־לְּךָ יְהוָה:	Yhwh will make a house for you.	Commissive
12	כִּי יִמְלְאוּ יָמֶיךָ וְשָׁכַבְתָּ אֶת־אֲבֹתֶיךָ וַהֲקִימֹתִי אֶת־זַרְעֲךָ אַחֲרֶיךָ אֲשֶׁר יֵצֵא מִמֵּעֶיךָ וַהֲכִינֹתִי אֶת־מַמְלַכְתּוֹ:	When your days are full and you lie down with your ancestors, I will raise up your offspring after you, who will come out from your insides, and I will establish his kingdom.	Commissives
13a	הוּא יִבְנֶה־בַּיִת לִשְׁמִי	He is the one who will build a house for my name.	Assertive
13b–15	וְכֹנַנְתִּי אֶת־כִּסֵּא מַמְלַכְתּוֹ עַד־עוֹלָם: אֲנִי אֶהְיֶה־לּוֹ לְאָב וְהוּא יִהְיֶה־לִּי לְבֵן אֲשֶׁר בְּהַעֲוֺתוֹ וְהֹכַחְתִּיו בְּשֵׁבֶט אֲנָשִׁים וּבְנִגְעֵי בְּנֵי אָדָם: וְחַסְדִּי לֹא־יָסוּר מִמֶּנּוּ כַּאֲשֶׁר הֲסִרֹתִי מֵעִם שָׁאוּל אֲשֶׁר הֲסִרֹתִי מִלְּפָנֶיךָ:	I will establish the throne of his kingdom permanently. I myself will be a father to him, and he will be a son to me. When he does wrong, I will rebuke him with a rod of mortals, with blows of human beings. But my commitment will not depart from him as I removed it from Saul, whom I removed from before you.	Commissives
16	וְנֶאְמַן בֵּיתְךָ וּמַמְלַכְתְּךָ עַד־עוֹלָם לְפָנֶיךָ כִּסְאֲךָ יִהְיֶה נָכוֹן עַד־עוֹלָם:	Your house and your kingdom will be secure permanently before you; your throne will be established permanently.	Assertives

he has gone, protecting him. With this description of the past and present as a foundation, God goes on to issue two commissives regarding divine future actions. Yhwh commits to making a great name for David (v. 9b) and to bringing security for Israel (v. 10a). This is followed by assertives that describe the world that Israel will experience as a result of Yhwh's actions (vv. 10b–11a), followed by another commissive ensuring security for David himself (11b). The speech acts in this section function by building upon each other; the opening assertives provide the foundation for Yhwh's commissives, which in turn provide the support for the hopeful world cast by the ensuing assertives and commissive.

Another speech formula signals the next group of speech acts (v. 11ca). In this section, Yhwh uses commissives to create the foundation for what follows. This foundation involves Yhwh's commitment to make a house for David (v. 11cb) by raising up an heir and establishing his kingdom (v. 12). This is followed by an assertive that indicates this heir will be the person who will build a house for Yhwh's name (v. 13a), followed by a series of commissives on how Yhwh will treat this individual (vv. 13b–15). God commits to adopting him and disciplining him when he does wrong, as well as remaining committed to him in a way that differs from Yhwh's treatment of David's predecessor, Saul. In this way, Yhwh invites David to envision a world in which Yhwh acts with commitment to David and his house that exceeds God's dealings with any previous royal family. This is further made clear by the final assertive in this group, which describes the permanency of David's house and kingdom (v. 16).

The narrator closes this section by sharing that Nathan spoke to David "in accordance with all these words and in accordance with this entire vision" (v. 17). Antony Campbell suggests that "as reported, God's promise can be reduced for David to three Hebrew words: a house I will build for you (*bayit 'ebneh lāk*)."[8] While this succinct summary adequately encapsulates God's promise, it fails to convey the strategic process by which Yhwh achieves this act of communication. The narrator's closing statement draws attention to the way in which "all these words" communicate an "entire vision," a description that fits well with the world-creating function of the speech acts that Yhwh gives to Nathan.

The response by David (vv. 18–29) demonstrates that the king's perspective has successfully been transformed by Yhwh's words. Now introduced by the narrator as "King David" (using both his title and his name), David performs a lengthy prayer that fits well with the world as it was portrayed by Yhwh's words. Van Wijk-Bos points out that "in this prayer, there is no mention of building a house for God."[9] Instead, King David refers to God as "my lord Adonai" seven times and to himself as "your servant" ten times. The opening lines speak only of the greatness of Adonai, who has done all these things for him. . . . From the praise of God, David segues into the praise of God's people, picking up on the themes of the divine speech.[10]

Van Wijk-Bos goes on to note that, "this is a David we will not meet again in what follows."[11] It is true that in the chapters that follow in 2 Samuel, David goes back to being portrayed as a complicated figure with characteristics and actions that fit both heroes and villains.[12] Nevertheless, it is also clear that, in this moment, David's perspective has been transformed by Yhwh's words.

On the story level, David performs directives to the prophet Nathan that draw attention to a discrepancy between the king's situation and that of Yhwh: the king resides in a house, but Yhwh only has a tent. While the king initially succeeds in obtaining Nathan's endorsement to build a temple, Yhwh soon interjects and directs Nathan to perform two groups of speech acts for David. The first group contains assertives and directives that resist the idea that Yhwh needs to live in a house. Yhwh directs David's attention to God's previous interactions with Israel, specifically how God had moved about in the tabernacle. After working to deconstruct the view that David must build a house for God, Yhwh proceeds to issue assertives and commissives that invite David to imagine a world in which Yhwh builds a house for David as well as a secure location in which Israel will live. The flexibility of usage in the word for "house" (בית) as a way to denote a physical structure but also a dynasty fits well with two competing ways of viewing the location of God's dwelling. While some may view God's dwelling place to be a physical location and a static structure, God transcends such limitations and actually lives in a dynamic way among God's people.

Storyteller Level

Interpreters have discussed possible purpose(s) for telling this story.[13] One prevalent viewpoint is that this story attempts to explain why David did not build the temple.[14] This view is compelling, especially given the way in which other passages also address this issue. For example, in the story found in 1 Chronicles 22, David tells Solomon that he had planned to build a house for Yhwh, but God had stopped him because he had shed much blood in his many wars (vv. 7–8). Solomon makes a similar claim when he sends a message to King Hiram of Tyre about the temple in 1 Kings 5:3. Here in 2 Samuel 7, Yhwh presses against the idea of David building him a temple because it does not fit with how God has previously acted with the Israelites. For audiences who are aware of a temple that is dedicated to Yhwh, this story shows that God only allowed it to be built, rather than initiating its construction.

This story enters into numerous intertextual conversations, including with other passages that speak of kings and temples. Interpreters who suggest that David has political benefits in mind with building a temple for Yhwh (on the story level) might find support for this possibility on the storyteller level. For example, when the northern kingdom of Israel separates from the southern kingdom of Judah in 1 Kings 12, King Jeroboam of Israel recognizes the political danger of allowing his subjects to continue to worship at the temple in Jerusalem.

> And Jeroboam said to himself, "Now the kingdom may return to the house of David. If this people go up to make sacrifices in the house of Yhwh in Jerusalem, the heart of this people will return to their lord, to Rehoboam, king of Judah. They will kill me and return to King Rehoboam of Judah." (1 Kgs. 12:26–27)

To avoid such a situation, Jeroboam creates two places of worship in the northern kingdom, one at Bethel and the other at Dan (see 1 Kgs 12:28–33).[15] Much later (around 160 years), when Amos prophesies against Israel at Bethel, the priest of Bethel reports him to the king and then attempts to drive Amos away (see Amos 7:10–17).

> And Amaziah said to Amos, "Seer, go! Flee for your life to the land of Judah. Eat bread there, prophesy there. Do not prophesy again at Bethel any more, because it is the king's sanctuary, and it is a temple (בית) of the kingdom." (Amos 7:12–13)

While Amos prophesies in the name of Yhwh, the priest views him as a political threat and speaks of the temple in Bethel only in its connection to the king.

Yhwh's response to having a temple in this passage also enters into intertextual conversations with texts that challenge the very idea of building a temple for Yhwh. For example, during Solomon's speech after building the temple, he acknowledges the tension involved with it when he says, "But will God truly dwell on the earth? See, the heavens and the highest heavens could not contain you, surely not this house that I have built" (1 Kgs. 8:27). A similar concept is found in the book of Isaiah in the context of rebuilding the temple:

> Thus says Yhwh: the heavens are my throne, and the earth is my footstool; where is a house that you would build for me, and where is my resting place? All these things my hand has made, and all these things are mine, declares Yhwh. (Isa. 66:1–2a)

Goldingay comments on these two passages, saying:

> Isaiah 66 thus begins by taking to its radical extreme the point Solomon makes. It portrays Yhwh in much bigger terms than happens when one speaks of a throne *in* the heavens and of the covenant chest as a footstool. In light of the fact that the whole cosmos is Yhwh's throne and the earth itself is Yhwh's footstool, the idea of building a house for Yhwh becomes nonsense.[16]

Goldingay goes on to suggest a key similarity between the temple and the monarchy in that both "entered Israel's story as a result of Israel's initiative rather than Yhwh's revelation. As the notion of human kingship makes no sense (because God is Israel's king), so the notion of an earthly temple makes no sense."[17] The temple, like the institution of human kingship, is presented in the books of Samuel as a concept that humans suggest and God allows. While other passages may celebrate Yhwh's relationship both with the king and the temple, their origin stories in the books of Samuel play an important role in understanding the limitations of these institutions for ancient Israel.

For audiences who construe this and other biblical narratives to be instructive for understanding God in their own world, this narrative might hold additional significance for understanding how God might interact with their own communities. For example, such a hermeneutic is evident when Craig Morrison notes the wordplay surrounding "house" in this passage and then says, "God seems to enjoy the wordplay. We should too."[18] In addition, for audiences who approach this story with the intention to learn about God, Yhwh's questions that are posed to David might make the audience think about limitations they too might have unconsciously imposed on how God might operate in their own lives. For example, Goldingay suggests similarities in Yhwh's response to David's idea of building a house for God with the biblical theme of the kingdom of God. He notes:

> One of my colleagues likes to remind people that Jesus never talks about our establishing God's kingdom or furthering it or building it or extending it. In the Gospels, the only things we do to God's kingdom are wait for it, see it, enter it, seek it, receive it, inherit it, and declare that it has come. In other words, we don't have an active relationship to it at all. In U.S. culture, this is an unpopular point to make, because people like to feel they can make a difference. . . . We don't like the fact that the gospel is about what God has done for us and not about what we do for God. (Yes, I know, we do have responsibility, and we are challenged to serve God and serve the world and so on, but we will not understand our role—and avoid disillusion—unless we see the point about the way Jesus talks.)[19]

Goldingay goes on to say that in this story, "David is our patron saint" in light of this reversal of how we want to act versus how God prefers to operate.[20]

Finally, Yhwh's response to David's temple proposal invites conversations involving the theological tension that exists between God's freedom and God's accessibility. David's initial assumption that Yhwh needs a house signals another outworking of what Brueggemann calls the "royal consciousness."[21] Since David has a house, he assumes that Yhwh needs a house. Pointing to the static nature of Solomon's temple as a key feature of his "economics of affluence" and "politics of oppression," Brueggemann suggests that "God and his temple have become part of the royal landscape, in which the sovereignty of God is fully subordinated to the purpose of the king."[22] He goes on to say, "God is now 'on call,' and access to him is controlled by the royal court."[23] For Brueggemann, the tension between the royal consciousness and the alternative imagination of Yhwh (and Moses and the prophets) offers a paradigm that extends throughout the Bible as well as beyond the biblical text. He says:

> In the imperial world of Pharaoh and Solomon, the prophetic alternative is a bad joke either to be squelched by force or ignored in satiation. But we are a haunted people because we believe the bad joke is rooted in the character of God himself, a God who is not the reflection of Pharaoh or of Solomon. He is a God with a name of his own, which cannot be uttered by anyone but him. He is not a reflection of any, for he has his own person and retains that all to himself. He is a God uncredentialed in the empire, unknown in the courts, unwelcome in the temple. And his history begins in his attentiveness to the cries of the marginal ones. He, unlike his royal regents, is one whose person is presented as passion and pathos, the power to care, the capacity to weep, the energy to grieve and then to rejoice. The prophets after Moses know that his caring, weeping, grieving, and rejoicing will not be outflanked by royal hardware or royal immunity because this one is indeed God. And kings must face that.[24]

Brueggemann's description of the way of imagining the world according to Pharaoh and Solomon also fit with the world that is cast by David's words as he first imagines Yhwh living in a temple rather than a tent. Similarly, Yhwh's response casts a vision that resists such a restricting of God's movement and accessibility. The extent of Brueggemann's paradigm may not yet be as evident in the exchange with David and Nathan as, for example, in the later stories of Solomon building the temple with forced labor (1 Kgs. 4:6; 5:13–16). Nevertheless, the presence of two competing ways of imagining God's freedom and accessibility in this story invites the audience to reflect on how their own viewpoints may fit more with the king or with God.

CONCLUSIONS

In 2 Samuel 7:1–17, the origin story of the temple and God's covenant with David exhibits different ways of imagining God's place and role among God's people. On the story level, the king initially views God to be someone who requires a house, like the king himself, and seeks permission from the prophet Nathan to start building the temple. Despite Nathan's initial approval, Yhwh rejects this plan and issues speech acts that demonstrate such a view of God's living space to be inconsistent with God's previous dealings with Israel. Instead, God issues speech acts for Nathan to perform for David that cast a different portrayal of where God dwells and how God interacts with people. After putting David's idea of a house in question, Yhwh goes on to commit to building a house for David. From a human perspective, Yhwh resides in a specific and static location to which those seeking God must come to interact with the divine. From a divine perspective, God does not dwell in a house but with a people. While God ultimately allows for a temple to be built, this is presented as an allowance rather than an ideal.

On the storyteller level, this narrative participates in numerous intertextual conversations involving various perspectives on the temple, as well as on ways in which God interacts with God's people. This story may also challenge audiences to question their own assumptions about God. Just as Yhwh offers a portrayal of the world that reverses how David imagines it, audiences who identify with David are invited to consider how God might work differently and even in opposition to their own expectations.

NOTES

1. Johanna W. H. van Wijk-Bos, *The Road to Kingship: 1-2 Samuel* (Grand Rapids: Eerdmans, 2020), 255.

2. Wijk-Bos, *The Road to Kingship*, 255.

3. Kevin J. Mellish, *1 & 2 Samuel: A Commentary in the Wesleyan Tradition* (Kansas City: Beacon Hill Press, 2012), 211.

4. Walter Brueggemann, *First and Second Samuel* (Louisville: John Knox Press, 1990), 254.

5. David Wolpe, *David: The Divided Heart* (New Haven: Yale University Press, 2014), 72.

6. Wijk-Bos, *The Road to Kingship*, 256–257.

7. Mellish, *1 & 2 Samuel*, 211.

8. Antony F. Campbell, *2 Samuel* (Grand Rapids: Eerdmans, 2005), 74.

9. Wijk-Bos, *The Road to Kingship*, 258; cf. Campbell, *2 Samuel*, 74.

10. Wijk-Bos, *The Road to Kingship*, 258.

11. Wijk-Bos, *The Road to Kingship*, 259.

12. As Wolpe succinctly states, "His story is like the Gestalt experiment: You can choose to see David as hero or knave." Wolpe, *David: The Divided Heart*, xii.

13. As with many scholarly discussions on Old Testament passages, many conversations have involved theories regarding a complicated literary history, with different sources and redactions attempting to impact their audiences in different ways. As with the other passages in the present study, the focus here will involve the impact(s) of the final form of the pericope.

14. For example, Alter says that "the author of this episode is faced with the difficulty of explaining a historical fact, that David did not build the temple, as we might have expected, but rather it was his son Solomon who carried out the construction." Robert Alter, *Ancient Israel: The Former Prophets: Joshua, Judges, Samuel, and Kings* (New York: W.W. Norton & Company, 2013), 462.

15. Richard Nelson calls Jeroboam's locations a "dark parallel to Solomon's temple." Richard D. Nelson, *First and Second Kings* (Louisville: Westminster John Knox Press, 2012), 81.

16. John Goldingay, *Isaiah 56–66 (ICC): A Critical and Exegetical Commentary* (London: Bloomsbury Publishing, 2014), 480.

17. Goldingay, *Isaiah 56–66*, 483. Goldingay points out that Isaiah 40–66 as a whole does not display any expectation that Yhwh will reestablish the monarchy, and says that instead, "Cyrus and/or the prophet and/or the people as a whole will now fulfil David's role (45.1; 52.14; 55.3–5; 61.1)."

18. Craig E. Morrison, *2 Samuel* (Collegeville, MN: Liturgical Press, 2013), 93.

19. John Goldingay, *1 and 2 Samuel for Everyone: A Theological Commentary on the Bible* (Louisville: Westminster John Knox Press, 2011), 133.

20. Goldingay, *1 and 2 Samuel for Everyone*, 133.

21. See the discussion of the royal consciousness as it pertains to Pharaoh's imagination and the oppression associated with totalizing regimes in chapter 4.

22. Brueggemann, *The Prophetic Imagination*, 28.

23. Brueggemann, *The Prophetic Imagination*, 29.

24. Brueggemann, *The Prophetic Imagination*, 36.

Chapter 7

Performative Prayers of a Prophet
(Jon. 2:1–10 [2–11]; 4:2–3)

Jonah is not typically known for his prayer life.[1] While interpreters of the book of Jonah have paid more attention to Jonah's (mis)adventure with a certain great fish and to his prophecy against a certain great city, both the great fish and the great city are the locations for Jonah's two prayers. Introduced by the narrator using the verb פלל, the first prayer appears near the end of the first act of the story (Jon. 2:1–9 [2–10])[2] and the second appears near the end of the second act (Jon. 4:2–3). The speech acts in both of Jonah's prayers utilize a chiastic structure to enhance their respective performative functions on both the story and storyteller levels. On the story level, Jonah's first prayer both celebrates and appeals to Yhwh's commitment (חֶסֶד) as he casts a world in which he himself is someone whom God is expected to save from trouble. In his second prayer, Jonah again highlights God's commitment as he explains his theological motivation for disobeying Yhwh's directive at the beginning of the story. On the storyteller level, these prayers highlight the importance of Yhwh's commitment (חֶסֶד) to God's identity and attempt to foster a hermeneutic of self-involvement within the audience that will enable them to view this book not merely as a story about Jonah but as a story about themselves.

JONAH'S FIRST PRAYER (JON. 2:1–9 [2–10])

Story Level

This passage opens with the narrator providing the speech situation for Jonah's prayer, saying, "And Jonah prayed to Yhwh his God from the belly of the fish, saying" (1–2aa [2–3ab]). The reference to the fish connects this prayer to the preceding narrative event of Yhwh appointing the great fish to swallow up Jonah. Reportedly, Jonah was in the belly of the fish for three days and three nights (Jon. 1:17 [2:1]), but the narrator does not specify when during these days and nights Jonah utters this speech act.

It has been widely recognized that the form of this prayer appears in the form of a psalm of thanksgiving (תּוֹדָה), and interpreters have noticed connections between this prayer and prayers within the book of Psalms.[3] Until recently, much of the scholarly discussion has concerned the issue of whether or not the prayer is secondary to the surrounding narrative.[4] The purpose here is not to prove or disprove that the psalm is secondary or original, but to investigate the function of the psalm at this point in the narrative.

The location for Jonah's prayer is the belly of the fish. While this is clear, the nature of this location, and thus his intended perlocutionary act, is debated by interpreters. Some view the appointment of the fish as a tool of Yhwh's deliverance of Jonah from drowning after being flung overboard. For example, George Landes asserts that "the fish has essentially a salvatory function" and says that it is obvious that the prayer "describes the plight of one—precisely like Jonah—about to be drowned in the sea."[5] Similarly, Douglas Stuart says that "the fish God designated rescued Jonah from death. Left in the sea, he would surely have drowned. Swallowed by the fish, he was preserved alive."[6] In this view, Jonah is recounting his experience of deliverance from drowning. Other interpreters have viewed the fish to be part of the trouble in which Jonah finds himself. Such a direction is followed by André and Pierre-Emmanuel Lacocque, who insist that the fish is not a saving device but rather belongs "to the awfulness of the sea."[7] This view might find support in the way that Jack Sasson translates the prayer using the present tense, as if it constitutes Jonah's present act of crying out to Yhwh in his trouble.[8] However, Landes notes that Jack Sasson's use of the present tense does not definitively answer the question of identification of Jonah's trouble.[9] Sasson himself tries to avoid what he calls the "unnecessary fixation with fish and their bellies."[10] A third option is presented by T. A. Perry, who says that the trouble from which Jonah first desires to be rescued is that of his life.[11] Calling Jonah's act of telling the sailors to hurl him into the sea as his attempted suicide, Perry says,

> This helps us understand that Jonah's first of two prayers is but a piece with his suicide or ongoing wish to die. In his "trouble" with this life or with God or whatever, he asks to be relieved of living and God obliges by casting him further into the depths into which he had already asked the sailors to lower him.[12]

As with the first position mentioned above, this third perspective views the fish as an answer to prayer, albeit a prayer for death rather than deliverance.

While all three interpretations of the speech situation regarding Jonah's "trouble" in v. 1 [2] can claim support from other aspects of the story level,

I am not persuaded by the idea that Jonah here wishes to die. Such an idea is present in Jonah's second prayer, but seems forced upon this first prayer, which as a whole celebrates Yhwh's deliverance. If Jonah begins by wishing to die, then he would need to change his mind during the prayer, an act that is not made conspicuous in the prayer itself.[13] Regarding the other two options, it is not necessary to decide whether Jonah wants to be delivered from the fish or whether he is thankful for the provision of the fish. Indeed, both of these could be true.

The speech acts of Jonah's first prayer form two chiastic structures: one beginning in v. 2ab [3ab] and extending through v. 7 [8] (see table 7.1), and the other starting in v. 8 [9] and extending through v. 9 [10] (see table 7.2).[14] He begins his prayer with two parallel assertives that describe his act of

Table 7.1

A – Assertives summarizing Jonah's cry, Yhwh's response (vv. 2ab–2b [3ab–3b])	קָרָאתִי מִצָּרָה לִי אֶל־יְהוָה וַיַּעֲנֵנִי מִבֶּטֶן שְׁאוֹל שִׁוַּעְתִּי שָׁמַעְתָּ קוֹלִי:	I called out of my trouble to Yhwh, and he answered me; out of the belly of Sheol I cried, you heard my voice.
B – Expressives concerning Yhwh's acts against Jonah (v. 3 [4])	וַתַּשְׁלִיכֵנִי מְצוּלָה בִּלְבַב יַמִּים וְנָהָר יְסֹבְבֵנִי כָּל־מִשְׁבָּרֶיךָ וְגַלֶּיךָ עָלַי עָבָרוּ:	You cast me (into) the depths, into the heart of the seas, and a river surrounded me; all your waves and your billows passed over me.
C – Assertive of Jonah's speech act (expressive and directive) (v. 4 [5])	וַאֲנִי אָמַרְתִּי נִגְרַשְׁתִּי מִנֶּגֶד עֵינֶיךָ אַךְ אוֹסִיף לְהַבִּיט אֶל־הֵיכַל קָדְשֶׁךָ:	Then I, I said, 'I have been driven away, from before your eyes; how will I look again at your holy temple?'
B' – Expressives describing results of Yhwh's acts against Jonah (vv. 5–6a [6–7a])	אֲפָפוּנִי מַיִם עַד־נֶפֶשׁ תְּהוֹם יְסֹבְבֵנִי סוּף חָבוּשׁ לְרֹאשִׁי: לְקִצְבֵי הָרִים יָרַדְתִּי הָאָרֶץ בְּרִחֶיהָ בַעֲדִי לְעוֹלָם	Waters encompassed me up to my neck; the deep surrounded me; reeds were wrapped around my head. To the foundations of the mountains I went down, the land whose bars were around me forever;
A' – Assertives that summarize Yhwh's response and Jonah's prayer (vv. 6b–7 [7b–8])	וַתַּעַל מִשַּׁחַת חַיַּי יְהוָה אֱלֹהָי: בְּהִתְעַטֵּף עָלַי נַפְשִׁי אֶת־יְהוָה זָכָרְתִּי וַתָּבוֹא אֵלֶיךָ תְּפִלָּתִי אֶל־הֵיכַל קָדְשֶׁךָ:	but you brought up my life from the Pit; O Yhwh my God. As my life was slipping away, I remembered Yhwh; and my prayer came to you, to your holy temple.

calling out to Yhwh out of his trouble, out of the belly of Sheol. In the center of the chiasm, Jonah will repeat the actual cry (v. 4 [5]), but here he shares the result of this speech act to involve Yhwh answering him and hearing his voice. While the precise situation of Jonah's trouble may not be entirely clear, it is evident that this prayer frames Jonah's situation as one of trouble, cry, and then rescue. It is also clear from these assertives that Jonah is committed to the idea that Yhwh is someone who can be called upon in times of trouble, and moreover that God is someone who will answer.

Following the assertive summarizing the act of deliverance, Jonah performs a speech act that further describes his situation of trouble. Whereas the assertive had spoken of Yhwh using the third person, here Jonah addresses his audience directly. Jonah tells Yhwh, "You cast me (into) the depths, into the heart of the seas" (v. 3a [4a]). The result of Yhwh's act against Jonah involves "a river surrounded me" and "all your waves and your billows passed over me" (v. 3b [4b]). Interpreters have noted that Jonah's description of his situation does not match the narrative. For example, John Holbert says, "Jonah is only half-right at most."[15] Phyllis Trible points out that "either his memory is faulty or his interpretation is skewed. He accuses Yhwh of casting him into the sea when in fact the sailors hurled him at his own request."[16] In the parlance of SAT, the direction of fit between the words and the narrative world is not appropriate for assertives. In fact, Jonah is not performing assertives at this point in his prayer. Unlike the third-person summary that begins his prayer, Jonah has now shifted his attention directly to Yhwh. He is not describing his situation as much as expressing to Yhwh what he feels in his situation. Thus, he is performing expressives rather than assertives. Unlike an assertive, an expressive does not utilize a direction of fit between words and the world; expressives can be successfully uttered without this criterion.[17] In other words, the truth of what Jonah is doing here should not be measured by its adherence to Jonah's world, but rather to his perception of his situation. For example, it may well be that Jonah attributes his entire situation to Yhwh (cf. Jon. 1:1–2, 4). While someone else might be able to remind Jonah of his own actions and the ways in which they contributed to his dire situation (Jon. 1:3; 2:12), Jonah himself might be unable to reflect on this at the moment.

In the midst of the expressives regarding his plight (B, B'), Jonah offers to Yhwh an assertive containing his prayer to God, a prayer within a prayer. Stuart suggests that the speech formula ואני אמרתי is best understood as a description of Jonah's thoughts rather than a report of an actual speech, and supports this idea by saying that this is a reference to Jonah's experience rather than a public declaration.[18] While Jonah is certainly expressing his view of his situation, he does, in fact, have a divine audience for this private speech act.

Located at the center of the first chiasm, this prayer proper is central to Jonah's larger prayer in both form and content, consisting of an expressive and a directive. The expressive that Jonah has been "driven away from before Yhwh's eyes" is followed by the directive, "How will I look again at your holy temple?" (Even if a question is intended to be rhetorical and thus does not require a direct response, it still functions as a directive in that it directs an audience to think.) With this expressive and accompanying directive, Jonah directs Yhwh to rescue him in a manner that is reminiscent of when the psalmist says to Yhwh in Psalm 6:4–5 [v. 5–6], "Turn, Yhwh, deliver me; save me for the sake of your commitment. For there is none among the dead who remember you. Who can give thanks to you in Sheol?" Such speech acts are not attempts to receive information, but to receive salvation.

The first chiasm is then completed with expressives and then assertives. The expressives in vv. 5–6a [6–7a] concern Jonah's perception of his situation, of being surrounded by waters, by the deep, and by reeds (B'). This situation is the result of the expressives concerning Yhwh's actions against Jonah in verse 3 [4] (B). But Jonah's description of his journey toward death shifts in verse 6b [7b] to assertives sharing of deliverance. Yhwh is described as having acted in response to Jonah's prayer (A'), completing the outer level of the chiasm that began with assertives in verse 2 [3].

After the first chiasm emphasizes Jonah's prayer (proper) to Yhwh, the second chiasm emphasizes a commissive that is surrounded by assertives that contrast Yhwh's faithfulness with the futility of following idols.

The first such assertive describes the futility of following idols by saying, "Those who keep worthless idols abandon their commitment" (v. 8 [9]). The precise meaning of this propositional content is not clear. Is this a description of pagans who abandon their commitment to their idols? Or, is this saying that the idol-worshipers are abandoning their true commitment, which is Yhwh?[19] The idea that they are abandoning Yhwh's commitment to them is appealing, but such an interpretation is better suited for the storyteller level than the story level (see below). Here it appears that Jonah is contrasting his commitment to Yhwh to the failed commitment of idol-worshipers to

Table 7.2

A—Assertive concerning those who keep idols (v. 8 [9])	מְשַׁמְּרִים הַבְלֵי־שָׁוְא חַסְדָּם יַעֲזֹבוּ׃	Those who keep worthless idols abandon their commitment.
B—Commissive by Jonah to Yhwh (v. 9a–ba [10a–ba])	וַאֲנִי בְּקוֹל תּוֹדָה אֶזְבְּחָה־לָּךְ אֲשֶׁר נָדַרְתִּי אֲשַׁלֵּמָה	But I with the voice of thanksgiving will sacrifice to you; that which I have vowed I will fulfill.
A'—Assertive concerning Yhwh (v. 9bb [10bb])	יְשׁוּעָתָה לַיהוה׃	Deliverance belongs to Yhwh!

their idols. On the story level, this assertive finds a match in the way that the sailors do not appear to be committed to their own gods in the storm and are quick to turn from their gods to Yhwh afterward. Any ambiguity of the first assertive (A) is countered with the clarity of the corresponding assertive (A'), "Deliverance belongs to Yhwh" (v. 9bb [10bb]). Commitments may differ, but Jonah shows that he believes there to be only one God who saves.

Centered within these assertives is Jonah's commissive to God that "I, with the voice of thanksgiving will sacrifice to you; that which I have vowed I will fulfill" (v. 9a–ba [10a–ba]). It may surprise the audience to see that Jonah does not connect his deliverance to an act of repentance, but to one of worship. In fact, the function of this commissive is to display Jonah as a faithful follower of Yhwh, someone who can expect Yhwh's deliverance.[20] Such an attitude fits with many prayers in the book of Psalms. As Goldingay points out, "It is more characteristic of prayer psalms to assert that one is not a faithless person . . . the spirituality of the Psalms is not dominated by sin in the way that Christian spirituality has been."[21] He goes on to say:

> Like Job, the Psalms themselves recognize that everyone is a sinner, but they focus more on the importance of the general orientation of one's life as involving commitment to God. . . . That is part of the basis for an appeal to Yhwh. If they are not so committed, then they had better not be praying at all but putting this right. Then they can praise and pray.[22]

In this prayer, Jonah is showing that he is someone who is committed to Yhwh and thus can expect Yhwh's commitment to extend to him during his time in the depths.

The two possibilities for the nature of Jonah's trouble (discussed above) contribute to an additional function of this commissive. If Jonah views the fish to be a saving device, then this commissive is uttered solely out of a desire to respond with thanksgiving. But if Jonah perceives that he is still in trouble, then this commissive additionally functions as a directive. This twofold view of the function of Jonah's prayer fits with the way in which Jonah places his directive and commissive at the center of their respective chiasms. What is more, the content of sacrificing to Yhwh in the commissive matches the cultic reference to the temple in the directive. If Jonah is trying to obtain deliverance from Yhwh as much as he is expressing his thanks, then this prayer certainly displays him to be the sort of person whom Yhwh would deliver.

On the story level, the act of portraying himself as a follower of Yhwh might be particularly important in Jonah's mind, as many of his actions thus far may leave the question open as to whether or not he is truly faithful to Yhwh. It may be that Jonah feels that Yhwh might need to be convinced of his level of commitment. Moreover, Yhwh's response to this prayer, directing the fish to vomit out Jonah on dry land, might further support such an interpretation of the perlocutionary function of this prayer. But even if Yhwh doesn't need to be convinced of Jonah's faithfulness, the audience might.[23]

Storyteller Level

Many interpreters have discussed ways in which this prayer contributes to the pace of the overall narrative as well as the structure, content, and message of the book. Trible points out that the psalm slows down the pace of the narrative, delaying the movement of the plot and thus extending the time that the audience must wait for resolution in a manner that is similar to Jonah waiting for three days and nights before he can resume his journey.[24] Lacocque and Lacocque have called this break in the action as "a kind of musical pause" and state that "if the psalm were not present at this point in the narrative, the tempo of the story as well as its configuration and meaning would be transformed."[25] Landes says,

> [W]e can see not only that the Jonah psalm is integral to the whole but also that it makes an essential contribution to the thought and message of the entire work. If it is removed, the symmetry between each major part is violated.[26]

He goes on to discuss the impact on the message: "In a very real sense, the concluding words of the Jonah psalm express the fundamental theme of the entire book: 'Salvation belongs to Yahweh!'"[27] The present study suggests that this prayer does more than contribute to the form and the content of the book; it also contributes to the performative function of the book.

On the storyteller level, the outer sections of the first chiasm perform an important function in fostering a hermeneutic of self-involvement that will draw the audience into viewing this prayer not only as Jonah's prayer but a prayer that they too can pray. The general nature of this prayer and even the incongruous nature of Jonah's expressives for his situation might enable readers to fill in the gaps and think of ways in which these assertive and expressives may fit their own situation. Jonah's description of his watery trouble holds many similarities to prayers in the book of Psalms. Notably, the exact phrase "all your waves and your billows passed over me," presumably in a figurative sense, appears in Psalm 42:8. One difference between Jonah's prayer and many of the psalms that use similar language is that, in Jonah's case, his situation can be viewed literally as well as metaphorically! The figurature use of these elements might enable the audience to see ways in which the world of Jonah might fit their world. Furthermore, the expressive that Jonah makes of himself as one who has been "driven away," while questionable on the story level, invites an audience who views themselves in this way to pray along.

The outer parts of the second chiasm also may involve the audience by leading them to consider the contrast between the futility of those who serve idols and those who can rely on Yhwh's commitment (חֶסֶד). Appearing twice in the book of Jonah (once in each of Jonah's prayers), חֶסֶד is a major theme in Scripture. Denoting faithfulness, love, loyalty, and devotion, חֶסֶד is often celebrated in the Old Testament within a covenantal context. However, it can also involve such commitment outside of any covenant relationship.[28] Prayers in the book of Psalms often speak of Yhwh's חֶסֶד, and it is striking that Psalm 42 speaks of Yhwh's חֶסֶד as well as all of Yhwh's billows and waves passing over the psalmist. An audience who is aware of the importance of חֶסֶד as a theme in Scripture is likely to fill in the gap concerning חֶסֶד in the second chiasm of this prayer and attribute true חֶסֶד to Yhwh. At the same time, for an audience who is unaware of Yhwh's חֶסֶד, this prayer informs them about Yhwh. As Limburg notes, "While most of the psalm speaks *to* the Lord, statements *about* the Lord are made in 2.2a, 7a, 9b, and, indirectly, 8 ("the one who loves them")."[29] On the storyteller level, the audience is invited to think of the חֶסֶד of Yhwh in this first prayer, even if here the חֶסֶד is overtly connected to false idols. Indeed, Yhwh's חֶסֶד will be addressed directly in Jonah's second prayer.

This prayer does more for the audience than speak about God; it invites the audience to utilize their newfound hermeneutic of self-involvement and to respond to God. Whereas the outer levels of the two chiasms invite the audience to consider Yhwh's חֶסֶד in their own time of trouble, the respective centers of the chiasms highlight Jonah's directive and commissive. The references to sacrifices also may signal that the audience themselves can worship Yhwh. Claus Westermann calls the todah (תּוֹדָה) psalms "Psalms of narrative praise by the individual" (he includes Jon. 2 in his list) and notes the inherent accompaniment of sacrifices offered in the temple.[30] He says that such a psalm, "presupposes the presence of a circle of listeners."[31] What Westermann says of the call to praise in Psalm 103:1–2 can be true of many, if not all, psalms in that they have the "remarkable capacity to evoke an echo in those who hear."[32] The same can be true of Jonah's first prayer.

One example of such an effect in reading prayers such as these is seen in the experience of Jürgen Moltmann. A prisoner of British prison camps from 1945 to 1948, an army chaplain had given Moltmann a New Testament that included the book of Psalms. Commenting that at the time he "would rather have had something to eat," Moltmann says that he became fascinated by the Psalms. "These psalms gave me the words for my own suffering," Moltmann writes. Reading the psalms would lead to his own experience of "not sinking into the abyss but of being held up from afar," which Moltmann says was the beginning of a clear hope.[33]

The first prayer of Jonah not only fosters a hermeneutic of involvement within the audience for the prayer alone, but it also invites them to place themselves within the larger narrative. On the storyteller level, this prayer changes the narrative from a story about a character named Jonah to a story that can also fit into the experience of the audience. An audience may resist this, of course, as the rest of the narrative contains content that few would want to embrace. In fact, the placement of this psalm at this point in the story may be an attempt to anticipate such resistance from the audience. Up until the prayer, it is likely that the audience has not identified with Jonah in hearing this narrative, even when he says that he is a Hebrew (1:9). Holbert notes that after the opening event of the book, "One cannot at this stage of the analysis claim that Jonah is a representative of anything or anybody other than himself."[34] This viewpoint is only slightly adjusted after the entire story unfolds, as Holbert sees the book of Jonah in its entirety as a satire that is written solely against "hypocritical prophets."[35] In this view, only hypocritical prophets and not the general audience are invited to utilize a hermeneutic of self-involvement when hearing the narrative. Other interpreters similarly maintain that the general audience should resist identifying themselves with Jonah but view him only as "the object of God's activity."[36] But the very fact that interpreters feel the need to direct audiences to stop identifying with Jonah shows that many readers are being drawn into the narrative. It is likely that readers do so after they hear Jonah's first prayer, which works to foster such a hermeneutic.

JONAH'S SECOND PRAYER (JON. 4:2–3)

Unlike his first prayer, this one is not in the poetic form of a psalm. However, it is similar to the first prayer in that the illocutionary acts form a chiasm (see table 7.3). Jonah begins and ends his prayer with expressives (A and A'), with the next level containing a combination of directives and expressives to Yhwh (B and B'). At the center of the chiasm are two assertives, one concerning Jonah's actions and the other concerning Yhwh's character as a direct reason for Jonah's actions (C and C').

Story Level

The narrator sets up the speech situation to involve a speaker (Jonah), an audience (Yhwh), and the emotional state of Jonah being angry (vv. 1–2a). This state of mind is further described in a way that indicates that this prayer is connected with the events that had just transpired in Nineveh in chapter 3. Jonah finds the situation displeasing (רעע) that God had changed his mind (נחם)

Table 7.3

A—Expressive (v. 2ba)	אַנָּה יהוה	Ah, Yhwh!
B—Directive / Expressive (v. 2bb)	הֲלוֹא־זֶה דְבָרִי עַד־הֱיוֹתִי עַל־אַדְמָתִי	Is this not what I said while I was in my own country?
C—Assertive (v. 2bc)	עַל־כֵּן קִדַּמְתִּי לִבְרֹחַ תַּרְשִׁישָׁה	This is why I fled the first time to Tarshish;
C'—Assertive (v. 2c)	כִּי יָדַעְתִּי כִּי אַתָּה אֵל־חַנּוּן וְרַחוּם אֶרֶךְ אַפַּיִם וְרַב־חֶסֶד וְנִחָם עַל־הָרָעָה:	because I knew that you are a gracious and compassionate God, slow to anger and abounding in commitment, one who relents concerning the disaster.
B'—Directive / Expressive (v. 3a)	וְעַתָּה יהוה קַח־נָא אֶת־נַפְשִׁי מִמֶּנִּי	And now, O Yhwh, please take my life from me,
A'—Expressive (v. 3b)	כִּי טוֹב מוֹתִי מֵחַיָּי:	for my death is better than my life.

about the disaster (רע) that he had said he would bring, after the entire city turned from their evil (רע) ways.

Jonah opens this prayer with an expressive ("Ah, Yhwh!") and then performs a question that functions both as an expressive and a directive. Jonah asks, "Is this not what I said while I was in my own country?" This question is a directive in that it prompts Jonah's audience, which on the story level is Yhwh, to consider the propositional content of the speech act. Like many questions, it may also be a directive for Yhwh to respond, and indeed God will do so. This question also functions as an expressive because its propositional content does not fit the narrative world. Jonah has not *said* this while he was in his own country, at least not in the narrative world as it is presented in the text. His response came in the form of the narrator describing Jonah's physical act of setting out to flee to Tarshish from the presence of Yhwh (see Jon. 1:3). If this speech act was only a directive for Yhwh to respond as to the direction of fit between Jonah's words and the narrative world, then Yhwh's response might be a simple, "No." But Yhwh will respond to Jonah's prayer as a whole as if it is an expressive ("Is it right for you to be angry?").

Jonah's ensuing assertives are central to his prayer in both form and content. Unlike the expressives in his first prayer that did not require a measurable direction of fit, these assertives are effective because they do fit the narrative world. Jonah says that his reason for disobeying Yhwh's directive to go to Nineveh and to cry out against it is based on his knowledge of Yhwh's character. Jonah speaks of Yhwh's character as "a gracious and compassionate God" as well as Yhwh's actions of being "slow to anger and abounding in commitment," someone who can be expected to relent (נחם) concerning disaster (רע).

While Jonah makes it clear that his reasoning had been theological, further details of his motivation remain hidden on the story level, leaving interpreters to fill in these details. Many interpreters have assumed that Jonah does not want his enemies to receive Yhwh's חֶסֶד. For example, Uriel Simon says,

> Jonah fled to Tarshish, instead of delivering the prophecy against Nineveh, because he was aware of the Lord's predisposition to mercy, so that the true purpose of the terrible verdict he was to proclaim to the inhabitants of the sinful city was to stimulate them to repent.[37]

Some readers suggest that Jonah's motivation may be more focused on himself than on his enemies. For example, J. J. M. Roberts suggests that Jonah is protecting his own reputation:

> If the city is not overthrown, Jonah's reputation will be hurt. By the criteria given in Deut 18:22, Jonah would be considered a presumptuous prophet. This was a constant source of anguish to the true prophets. They did not want to see the punishment of their people which they were called upon to predict, but if the fulfillment of their predictions were delayed, the very people they were trying to save would make fun of them.[38]

This interpretation fits with Eagleton's earlier suggestion that "what happens in Nineveh is exactly what Jonah feared all along: that God's own chronic self-deception would drag him into its own wake and leave him looking a complete idiot."[39] On the story level, perhaps Jonah is the only one who can explain the reason why his knowledge of Yhwh's compassion led to his own disobedience. Or, perhaps Jonah himself needs to reflect on this.

Jonah ends his brief prayer as it had begun, with a combination of expressive and directive, "And now O Yhwh, please take my life from me, for my death is better than my life" (v. 3). This ending to his prayer opens up a conversation with Yhwh, whether Jonah intends for this or not. Whereas Jonah's first prayer had been followed by Yhwh speaking to the great fish (Jon. 2:11 [10]), Yhwh here speaks to Jonah with a directive, "Is it right for you to be angry?" Jonah's nonverbal response to this question might signal that he does not want to continue the conversation.[40] Nevertheless, Yhwh remains engaged and initiates a scenario for Jonah that becomes an object lesson involving a plant and then a worm that afflicts it (vv. 6–8), culminating in Jonah once again requesting death. As before, God directs Jonah to reflect on his anger: "Is it right for you to be angry concerning the bush?" (v. 9a). This time, Jonah responds with an assertive, affirming that his anger in regard to the death of the plant is indeed appropriate (v. 9b). In response, Yhwh compares Jonah's valid concern for the plant with God's own concern for the city of Nineveh including all of its many human and animal inhabitants (vv. 10–11).[41]

Whether Jonah's motivation is spiteful or selfish, the conversation that ensues after his prayer shows that Yhwh tries to help Jonah view the situation from a divine perspective. Indeed, Eagleton appeals to speech act theory (SAT) to suggest that what has occurred in Nineveh was God's plan all along. He says,

> God's view of the matter, of course, is that it's *because* Jonah has cried doom that the doom hasn't come. The only successful prophet is an ineffectual one, one whose warnings fail to materialize. All good prophets are false prophets, undoing their own utterances in the very act of producing them.[42]

Houston has suggested that Eagleton's description of the function of prophecy fits with the case of Jonah but may be overdrawn in light of other uses of prophetic announcements.[43] Nevertheless, this conversation shows that Yhwh's illocutionary act of pronouncing judgment against Nineveh constitutes a divine perlocutionary act of directing Nineveh to repent and find mercy. Jonah has been used by God to achieve this purpose, even though Jonah himself may not share in God's desire to bring it about.

Storyteller Level

On the storyteller level, this prayer performs at least three tasks. First, this prayer highlights certain characteristics of Yhwh. Several other passages in Scripture describe Yhwh as someone who is "a gracious and compassionate God," someone who is "slow to anger and abounding in commitment," as well as someone who can be expected to relent concerning disaster.[44] A dominant aspect of the Old Testament's testimony of God, the audience can view the practical nature of this theology in the context of a narrative and see that it is not reserved for Israel. "The story of Jonah makes it clear that this steadfast love is not limited to God's own people."[45] Yhwh is portrayed not only as someone who acts with commitment for his own people but for the entire world. This theology is emphasized here as being integral to the plot of the story as a whole.

A second function of this prayer is that it creates a contrast between this compassionate God and this spiteful prophet. Such a distancing between Yhwh and Jonah may serve as an invitation for an audience to respond to Yhwh despite being rejected by Yhwh's people. In fact, this story may even be told with such an audience in mind. As Limburg points out:

> One cannot miss the positive portrayal of the non-Israelites, the "people of the world" in the story. The sailors along with their captain are men of piety and action (1:5-6), decent human beings (1:12-14) who are eager to do the right thing in the eyes of a God about whom they have heard little (1:14). They finally

come to worship that God (1:16). After only a few words from the prophet Jonah about the corrupt state of their city, the people of Nineveh and their king, even their animals, all engage in sincere acts of repentance and turn their life-styles around. (Jon. 3)[46]

Such elements are viewed by Holbert to contribute to the satirical element of the book.[47] But the viewpoint that these characters are satirical would only be evident to an audience that holds expectations that differ from this textual world. An audience who identifies with these outsiders might be drawn into the story by these surprising elements. This positive act of repentance would be performed in spite of Jonah's negative prayer, leading to an impact on the storyteller level that is as wonderfully ironic and felicitous for Yhwh's purposes as it has been on the story level!

A third function is evident for the audience who has accepted the invitation to utilize a hermeneutic of self-involvement from Jonah's first prayer. Interpreters who apply synchronic methods have long noticed ways in which Jonah's two prayers work together by contributing to the overall structure and content of the book of Jonah.[48] They also work together for the function of these prayers. Following a study by Wolff on the impact of the many questions contained in the book of Jonah, Limburg says, "If a story is skillfully told, the storyteller can use questions to put each listener in the place of the one being questioned."[49] One contribution of the present study is to suggest that Jonah's first prayer functions to help the audience place themselves in this position. An audience who has identified with Jonah's previous prayer of thanksgiving for Yhwh's mercy might consider Jonah's prayer for Yhwh's judgment against the petitioner's enemies. The book of Psalms invites the audience to pray both of these types of prayers (Jonah is not wrong to pray honestly when he is angry), and here in Jonah the audience is invited to see the exchange between Yhwh and Jonah that this prayer initiates. On the storyteller level, the audience might decide for themselves whether Jonah has acted out of animosity for his enemies, out of self-preservation, or both. Such a decision likely would indicate the audience's own motivation as much as their perception of Jonah's decision.

All this might be a shock for the audience, and may be met with resistance. After all, it is difficult to listen to a story in which your enemy receives the sort of compassion and deliverance that Yhwh has given to you. Such an attitude can be seen in modern interpreters—Jonah is not alone in his anger about God forgiving Nineveh![50] Many interpreters choose to express their affirmation of Jonah's initial prophecy against Nineveh, and others are quick to bring up the message of the book of Nahum as proof that the mercy shown to Nineveh in the book of Jonah is short-lived. This is precisely the sort of

audience that the book of Jonah invites to pray these prayers and to listen to
Yhwh's exchange with Jonah in chapter 4. It is no accident that the book ends
with a question that is as much for the listening audience as it is for Jonah.

CONCLUSIONS

The present investigation has demonstrated that the two prayers of Jonah
relate to the narrative world as well as to the function of the book as a whole.
On the story level, the first prayer casts a world in which Jonah is a faithful follower of Yhwh, despite his act of disobedience at the beginning of
the story. Jonah seeks and celebrates Yhwh's commitment and deliverance.
The second prayer opens up a conversation with Yhwh as Jonah reveals his
motivation for initially disobeying the divine directive. On the storyteller
level, these prayers emphasize Yhwh's commitment (חֶסֶד), showing Yhwh to
be faithful not only to his followers but to the whole world. What is more,
the first prayer attempts to foster a hermeneutic of self-involvement within
the audience so that they begin to identify with Jonah instead of distancing
themselves from this character. An audience who identifies with Jonah's first
prayer may consider ways they can relate to his second prayer, the ensuing
conversation with Yhwh, and the story as a whole. By including these two
prayers in the narrative, the book of Jonah becomes an invitation for all readers to respond to Yhwh's amazing commitment.

NOTES

1. A previous version of this chapter was published as Steven T. Mann, "Performative Prayers of a Prophet: Investigating the Prayers of Jonah as Speech Acts,"
Catholic Biblical Quarterly 79 (2017): 20–40. Used by permission.

2. The verse numbers in the Hebrew text are given in brackets.

3. See especially James Limburg, *Jonah* (Louisville: Westminster John Knox
Press, 1993), 63–64.

4. For an overview of the discussion regarding the interpolative character of the
prayer, see John C. Holbert, "'Deliverance Belongs to Yahweh!' Satire in the Book
of Jonah," *Journal for the Study of the Old Testament* 21 (1981): 59–81.

5. George M. Landes, "The Kerygma of the Book of Jonah: The Contextual
Interpretation of the Jonah Psalm," *Interpretation* 21 (1967): 3–31 (13).

6. Douglas Stuart, *Hosea–Jonah* (Nashville: Thomas Nelson, 1987), 472. cf.
Limburg, *Jonah,* 60.

7. André Lacocque and Pierre-Emmanuel Lacocque, *The Jonah Complex*
(Atlanta: John Knox Press, 1981), 53. Here they purportedly draw on Landes
("The Kerygma of the Book of Jonah," 12–13). However, Landes disputes this use
of his article. See George M. Landes, Review of *Jonah: A New Translation with*

Introduction, Commentary, and Interpretation, by Jack M. Sasson, and *Jonah* of *Jonah: A Psycho-Religious Approach to the Prophet,* by André Lacocque and Pierre-Emmanuel Lacocque, *Journal of Biblical Literature* 111, no. 1 (1992): 130–34 (132–33). Indeed, Landes ("The Kerygma of the Book of Jonah," 12–13) states,

> By having Jonah swallowed by the fish, the writer had therefore no intention of implying it was the cause of the prophet's distress, or even that it was a vehicle of punitive judgment upon him. The fish, "appointed" by Yahweh, is simply a beneficent device for returning Jonah to the place where he may reassume the commission he had previously abandoned.

8. Jack Sasson, *Jonah: A New Translation with Introduction, Commentary, and Interpretation* (New York: Doubleday, 1990), 160.

9. Landes, Review of *Jonah*, 131.

10. Sasson, *Jonah*, 168.

11. T. A. Perry, *The Honeymoon Is Over: Jonah's Argument with God* (Peabody, MA: Hendrickson, 2006), 11–12, 23–24.

12. Perry, *The Honeymoon Is Over*, 24. Uriel Simon also views Jonah's directive for the sailors to throw him into the sea as a suicide attempt, saying, "He chooses death—passive suicide (cf. Judg. 9:54 and 16:30; 1 Sam. 31:4)—to abandoning his flight and prophesying against Nineveh." Uriel Simon, *Jonah* (Philadelphia: Jewish Publication Society, 1999), 13.

13. Perry (*The Honeymoon Is Over*, 24, 29) says that God "calls his bluff" and that Jonah immediately changes his mind once he is in the depths and then prays for deliverance. Then "Jonah ends up thanking God for *not* answering his prayer to die."

14. The idea that this prayer is structured as a chiasm is not new to interpreters, as various possible chiastic structures have been identified. See, for example, Phyllis Trible, *Rhetorical Criticism: Content, Method, and the Book of Jonah* (Minneapolis: Fortress, 1994), 163–73; Sasson, *Jonah,* 167.

15. Holbert, "Deliverance Belongs to Yahweh," 71.

16. Trible, *Rhetorical Criticism*, 167–68.

17. See Searle, *Expression and Meaning*, 12–20.

18. Stuart, *Jonah*, 468–69; cf. Landes, "The Kerygma of the Book of Jonah," 7.

19. For an example of the latter interpretation, see Limburg, *Jonah*, 64. Cf. this verse in the NIV: "Those who cling to worthless idols turn away from God's love for them."

20. Against Hill and Walton, who say that this prayer shows that "Jonah fully recognizes himself as an undeserving recipient of God's grace." Andrew Hill and John Walton, *A Survey of the Old Testament*, 2nd ed. (Grand Rapids: Zondervan, 2000), 501.

21. John Goldingay, *Psalms* (Baker Commentary on the Old Testament; Grand Rapids: Baker Academic, 2006), 64.

22. Goldingay, *Psalms*, 64.

23. For example, Trible (*Rhetorical Criticism*, 168) points to the dissonance between the way Jonah is portrayed in the narrative and the way that he is portrayed in his prayer. She says, "The cultic piety avowed hardly fits Jonah's demeanor. Such dissonance drives wedges between the psalm and the narrative—or it makes

grotesque the developing portrait of Jonah." Stuart (*Jonah*, 472–73) suggests that the discrepancy shows that Jonah has undergone a "partial change of heart that caused him to be willing to obey the command of God when it came to him a second time."

24. Trible, *Rhetorical Criticism*, 162.

25. Lacocque and Lacocque, *The Jonah Complex*, 52.

26. Landes, "The Kerygma of the Book of Jonah," 29–30.

27. Landes, "The Kerygma of the Book of Jonah," 29–30.

28. Both connotations are present in the book of Ruth. For example, Orpah and Ruth have shown *hesed* to their husbands and to Naomi within a covenant relationship. In Ruth 3:10, Ruth shows *hesed* to Boaz without a covenant relationship. In the book of Daniel (1:9), the *hesed* that the officer in charge shows is displayed when he had no obligation to display such a commitment to Daniel.

29. Limburg, *Jonah,* 66.

30. Claus Westermann, *The Psalms: Structure, Content & Message* (trans. Ralph D. Gehrke; Minneapolis: Augsburg Publishing House, 1980), 72–73.

31. Westermann, *The Psalms*, 73.

32. Westermann, *The Psalms*, 5.

33. Jürgen Moltmann, *Experiences of God* (Philadelphia: Fortress Press, 1980), 6–9.

34. Holbert, "Deliverance Belongs to Yahweh," 59.

35. Holbert, "Deliverance Belongs to Yahweh," esp. pp. 74–75.

36. E.g., Hill and Walton (*A Survey of the Old Testament,* 499) say, "The book is not using Jonah to represent Israel and thereby urging action (e.g., evangelize, forgive, be compassionate, etc.). Rather, it is identifying all three (Jonah, Nineveh, and Israel) as the object of God's activity."

37. Simon, *Jonah*, 35.

38. J. J. M. Roberts, *The Bible and the Ancient Near East* (Winona Lake: Eisenbrauns, 2002), 409–10. Roberts goes on to point to Jeremiah's bitter lament in Jeremiah 17:14–18.

39. Terry Eagleton, "J.L. Austin and the Book of Jonah," *New Blackfriars* 69 (1988): 164–68 (165).

40. Limburg says that "Jonah responds to the Lord's question by walking out on the discussion." Limburg, *Jonah*, 94.

41. Yhwh's final utterance in the book of Jonah is predominantly understood by interpreters as a rhetorical question, which therefore functions as a directive for Jonah to consider Yhwh's concern for the great city of Nineveh and its many human and animal inhabitants. Recently, some interpreters have challenged this interpretation by pointing out that this utterance is not clearly presented as a question in Hebrew. For example, Erickson says, "grammatically, reading God's reply as a declarative statement ('But I am not concerned about Nineveh . . .') represents the plain sense reading." Amy Erickson, *Jonah Introduction and Commentary* (Grand Rapids: Eerdmans, 2021), 406. Obviously, such a construal of Yhwh's final utterance leads to a drastically different perception of the function of Yhwh's speech act on the story level and the function of this exchange on the storyteller level (e.g., see Erickson, *Jonah*, 413–14). For a helpful discussion of this issue and a defense for continuing to interpret this utterance as a question, see "Excursus 8: Question or Assertion? The

Ending of Jonah in 4:11" on pages 296–98 in Rhiannon Graybill, John Kaltner, and Steven L. McKenzie, *Jonah: A New Translation with Introduction and Commentary* (New Haven: Yale University Press, 2023).

42. Eagleton, "J.L. Austin and the Book of Jonah," 165–66.

43. Walter J. Houston, "What Did the Prophets Think They Were Doing? Speech Acts and Prophetic Discourse in the Old Testament," *Biblical Interpretation* 1 (1993): 167–88 (183).

44. For a concise and helpful overview of this language in the Old Testament, see Limburg, *Jonah*, 90.

45. Limburg, *Jonah*, 92.

46. Limburg, *Jonah*, 35.

47. Holbert, "Deliverance Belongs to Yahweh."

48. For example, Landes ("The Kerygma of the Book of Jonah," 16–17) sees parallel motifs between the psalm in chapter 2 and portions of chapter 4, even though they differ from each other in form, type, and content. "Within the over-all structure of the Book of Jonah, the psalm is placed directly parallel to the prophet's prayer in 4:2–3."

49. Limburg, *Jonah*, 25.

50. For example, see the list of interpreters who are alleged to express their affirmation of Jonah's initial prophecy against Nineveh in Lacocque and Lacocque, *The Jonah Complex*, 82.

Chapter 8

How to Do Things with Worlds

When considering the possibility of words creating worlds in biblical narrative, we might initially assume that only God (on the story level) and the narrator (storyteller level) can perform this feat. God might create an aspect of the story's world by performing a divine declarative such as "Let there be" while a storyteller's words bring the very elements of a narrative world into existence within the imagination of the audience. This study has demonstrated that human characters can also create worlds with their words in a manner that is similar to storytellers. All characters can perform speech acts that utilize a world-from-words direction of fit as they attempt to impact other characters. The present study has also affirmed that the act of storytelling can create a narrative world that may endorse, condemn, or highlight the worlds that are created by the characters' words.

The investigation of the Cain-oriented speech acts in Genesis 4 (see chapter 2) provides two basic categories for organizing the worlds that are created by characters in the other passages explored in this book. On one side, Eve and Yhwh project worlds that celebrate God's relationship with humanity and resist human sin and violence. On the other side, Cain and Lamech speak of worlds that reject this notion and choose to focus only on themselves. A similar clash between worlds is on display in the conflicting views of the land presented by the reports of the spies in Numbers 13–14. On one side, the Israelites can view the land as a gift from Yhwh and trust that God will protect them; the other side looks at the land with fear of insurmountable threats without considering the impact of God's presence. The toxic imagination of Cain and Lamech also appears in a concentrated form in Exodus 1:8–22, as Pharaoh uses his words to influence the Egyptians' imagination and incite oppression and violence as he advances his own selfish interests. The intercessory prayers of Abraham, Moses, and Amos attempt to direct God's attention away from aspects of the world that may fit with Cain and Lamech, and toward worlds that fit into the category of Eve and Yhwh.

Characters can also create worlds that are more nuanced in their classification. For example, God counters the world that is cast by David's proposal to build a temple for Yhwh by performing speech acts that depict a world in which such an act will be allowed but not fully endorsed. God then commits to building a house for David, shifting the perspective away from the human king's authority to a world in which Yhwh exhibits freedom that is uninhibited by human constraints. In this way, God issues a corrective to a character's world without dismantling it completely.

While many (but not all) of the worlds created by the characters in these passages can be organized into two distinct groups, the utilizations of these worlds are not limited by their category. The midwives view the world from a perspective of fearing Yhwh and not Pharaoh, but they utilize the toxic world created by Pharaoh's words to protect themselves from his wrath after they resist the king's directive. Rather than offering an opposing world to the king, they appeal to an aspect of his own world in a way that dismantles his schemes. Another example of the flexible usage of worlds is evident from the prayers that are presented in this study. All of these prayers project worlds that fit into the category that emphasizes and celebrate God's gracious relationship with humanity. While the intercessory prayers of Abraham, Moses, and Amos use these worlds to divert God's wrath away from others, Jonah appeals to these worlds in prayers that attempt to receive God's grace for himself and to defend his attempt to withhold it from others.

Narrative worlds also have performative power on the storyteller level, both in regard to the individual worlds that are offered by characters, and to the overarching world of the story. Some of these worlds are explicitly instructive, offering practical examples that enable audiences to understand and apply theological truths. For example, the midwives' story offers a tangible outworking of how to implement the "fear" of God to protect those who are vulnerable. The clashing reports of the spies in Numbers 13–14 demonstrate the importance for God's people to make decisions that trust God; when they fail, the ensuing intercession by Moses and Yhwh's response provide a concrete example of Scripture's complex portrayal of Yhwh as someone who is both compassionate and tough.[1] The successful use of imaginary worlds to promote the aims of intercessory prayers in these stories might offer guidance to audiences who themselves perform such prayers. In such cases, there is evidence to suggest that the storytellers have structured the narratives to intentionally promote the adoption and usage of certain viewpoints.

Narrative worlds can also impact audiences in more subtle ways. For interpreters who approach these texts as Scripture and seek to apply biblical truths in their own situations, the intertextual relationships on display between these worlds might encourage them to seek out more than one perspective within biblical texts. Readers who view the world differently than the characters or storytellers might find it fruitful to engage in conversation with these texts as they consider the possible benefits and liabilities involved with all of the worlds represented (including their own). The diversity of worlds on display in these texts might also invite audiences to engage not only in intertextual conversations but discussions with other interpreters who may see the world differently.

In his 1916 essay entitled "The Strange New World Within the Bible," Karl Barth speaks of the Bible as a doorway to another country that readers enter when they open its pages.[2] Noting that modern readers might be surprised at the strange attitudes and actions of biblical characters, he nevertheless encourages readers to "find God in the Bible."[3] This study has shown that the Old Testament offers countless worlds for readers to explore, including those that display a variety of perspectives concerning the identity and character of God. Spending time in a foreign country can be a transformative experience, simply due to the exposure to different ways of thinking and acting. In a similar way, readers of these ancient texts might find that their exposure to the narrative worlds of the Old Testament will result in a transformed imagination that opens new perspectives within their own world.

NOTES

1. For a helpful discussion of these two aspects of God's character in Exodus 34:6–7, see John Goldingay, *An Introduction to the Old Testament: Exploring Text, Approaches and Issues* (London: SPCK, 2016), 96–97.

2. Karl Barth, "The Strange New World Within the Bible," in *A Map of Twentieth-Century Theology: Readings from Karl Barth to Radical Pluralism,* eds. R. Jenson and C. E. Braaten (Minneapolis: Fortress Press, 1995).

3. Barth, "The Strange New World," 30.

Bibliography

Alter, Robert. *The Five Books of Moses: A Translation with Commentary.* New York: W.W. Norton & Company, 2004.

————. *Ancient Israel: The Former Prophets: Joshua, Judges, Samuel, and Kings: A Translation with Commentary.* New York: W.W. Norton & Company, 2013.

Andersen, Francis I. and A. Dean Forbes. *The Hebrew Bible: Andersen-Forbes Analyzed Text,* Logos Research Edition, 2008.

Austin, John Langshaw. "Performative Utterances." In *Philosophical Papers,* edited by J. O. Urmson and G. J. Warnock, 233–41. Oxford: Clarendon Press, 1970. Reprinted in *Philosophy of Language: The Big Questions,* edited by Andrea Nye, 126–31. Malden, MA: Blackwell Publishers, 1998.

————. *How to Do Things With Words.* Edited by J. O. Urmson and Marina Sbisà. Cambridge, MA: Harvard University Press, 1975.

Barth, Karl. "The Strange New World Within the Bible." In *A Map of Twentieth-Century Theology: Readings from Karl Barth to Radical Pluralism,* edited by R. Jenson and C. E. Braaten. Minneapolis: Fortress Press, 1995.

Ben Zvi, Ehud. "The Dialogue Between Abraham and YHWH in Gen 18:23–32: A Historical-Critical Analysis." *Journal for the Study of the Old Testament* 17 (1992): 27–46.

Birch, Bruce C., Walter Brueggemann, Terence E. Fretheim, and David L. Petersen. *A Theological Introduction to the Old Testament,* 2nd ed. Nashville: Abingdon Press, 2011.

Boesak, Allan. *Black and Reformed: Apartheid, Liberation, and the Calvinist Tradition.* Edited by Leonard Sweetman. Maryknoll, NY: Orbis Books, 1984.

Brett, Mark G. *Decolonizing God: The Bible in the Tides of Empire.* Sheffield: Sheffield Phoenix Press, 2008.

Bridge, Edward. "Abraham's Dialogue with God in Genesis 18." *Journal for the Study of the Old Testament* 40 (2016): 281–96.

Briggs, Richard. "The Uses of Speech-Act Theory in Biblical Interpretation." *Currents in Research* 9 (2001): 229–76.

Brown, Francis, Samuel Rolles Driver, and Charles Augustus Briggs. *Enhanced Brown-Driver-Briggs Hebrew and English Lexicon.* Oxford: Clarendon Press, 1977.

Brown, Jeannine K. *Scripture as Communication: Introducing Biblical Hermeneutics.* Grand Rapids: Baker Academic, 2021.

Bruckner, James K. *Exodus.* Peabody, MA: Hendrickson, 2008.

Brueggemann, Walter. *The Land: Place as Gift, Promise, and Challenge in Biblical Faith.* Philadelphia: Fortress Press, 1977.

———. *First and Second Samuel.* Louisville: John Knox Press, 1990.

———. *Theology of the Old Testament: Testimony, Dispute, Advocacy.* Minneapolis: Fortress Press, 1997.

———. *The Prophetic Imagination,* 2nd ed. Minneapolis: Fortress Press, 2001.

———. *Spirituality of the Psalms.* Minneapolis: Fortress Press, 2002.

———. *Great Prayers of the Old Testament.* Louisville: Westminster John Knox Press, 2008.

———. *Divine Presence Amid Violence: Contextualizing the Book of Joshua.* Eugene, OR: Cascade Books, 2009.

———. "Testimony that Breaks the Silence of Totalism." *Interpretation* 70, no. 3 (2016): 275–87.

Byron, John. *Cain and Abel in Text and Tradition: Jewish and Christian Interpretations of the First Sibling Rivalry.* Leiden: Brill, 2011.

Camp, Phillip G. "Prayer in the Pentateuch." In *Praying with Ancient Israel Exploring the Theology of Prayer in the Old Testament*, edited by Phillip G. Camp and Tremper Longman III, 21–36. Abilene: Abilene Christian University Press, 2015.

Campbell, Antony F. *2 Samuel.* Grand Rapids: Eerdmans, 2005.

Cassuto, Umberto. *A Commentary on the Book of Genesis: Part 1 – From Adam to Noah, Genesis I–VI8.* Translated by Israel Abrahams. Jerusalem: Magnes, 1961.

Chatman, Seymour. *Story and Discourse: Narrative Structure in Fiction and Film.* Ithaca: Cornell University, 1978.

Childs, Brevard. *The Book of Exodus.* Louisville: The Westminster Press, 1974.

Chisholm Jr., Robert B. "Anatomy of an Anthropomorphism: Does God Discover Facts?" *Bibliotheca Sacra* 164 (2007): 3–20.

Coats, George. *Rebellion in the Wilderness: The Murmuring Motif in the Wilderness Traditions of the Old Testament.* Nashville: Abingdon Press, 1968.

Cotter, David W. *Genesis.* Collegeville, MI: The Liturgical Press, 2003.

De Groot, Christiana. "Genesis." In *The IVP Women's Bible* Commentary, edited by Catherine Clark Kroeger and Mary J. Evans, 1–27. Downers Grove: IVP, 2002.

Dohmen, C. and D. Rick. "רעע." In *Theological Dictionary of the Old Testament,* edited by Helmer Ringgren, et al., 561–88. Grand Rapids: Eerdmans, 2004.

Dorn, Louis. "'Lo' and 'behold' – Translating the Hebrew Word Hinney." *Biblical Translator* 52 (2001): 222–29.

Dozeman, Thomas B., Konrad Schmid, and Baruch J. Schwartz, eds. *The Pentateuch: International Perspectives on Current Research.* Tubingen: Mohr Siebeck, 2011.

Eagleton, Terry. "J.L. Austin and the Book of Jonah." *New Blackfriars* 69 (1988): 164–68.

Erickson, Amy. *Jonah Introduction and Commentary.* Grand Rapids: Eerdmans, 2021.

Evans, Donald. *The Logic of Self-Involvement: A Philosophical Study of Everyday Language with Special Reference to the Christian Use of Language about God as Creator.* London: SCM Press, 1963.

Exum, Cheryl J. "'You Shall Let Every Daughter Live': A Study of Exodus 1:82:10." *Semeia* 28 (1983): 63–82.

Freedman, David Noel. "When God Repents." In *Divine Commitment and Human Obligation: Selected Writings of David Noel Freedman,* edited by John R. Huddlestun, 409–46. Grand Rapids: Eerdmans, 1997.

Fretheim, Terence. *The Suffering of God: An Old Testament Perspective.* Philadelphia: Fortress Press, 1984.

Frymer-Kensky, Tikva. *Reading the Women of the Bible.* New York: Schocken Books, 2002.

Fuhs, H. F. "רָאָה." In *Theological Dictionary of the Old Testament,* edited by Helmer Ringgren, et al., 290–315. Grand Rapids: Eerdmans, 1990.

Gafney, Wilda C. *Womanist Midrash: A Reintroduction to the Women of the Torah and the Throne.* Louisville: Westminster John Knox Press, 2017.

Galambush, Julie. "'ādām from 'ădāmâ, 'iššâ from 'îš: Derivation and Subordination in Genesis 2:4b–3:24." In *History and Interpretation: Essays in Honour of John H. Hayes,* edited by M. Patrick Graham, et al., 33–46. Sheffield: Sheffield Academic Press, 1993.

———. *Reading Genesis: A Literary and Theological Commentary.* Macon, GA: Smyth & Helwys Publishing, 2018.

Goldingay, John. *Models for Interpretation of Scripture.* Toronto: Clements, 1995.

———. Introduction to Rogerson, John, R.W.L. Moberly and William Johnstone, *Genesis and Exodus.* Sheffield: Sheffield Academic Press, 2001.

———. *Isaiah.* Understanding the Bible Commentary Series. Grand Rapids: Baker Books, 2001.

———. *Old Testament Theology, Volume One: Israel's Gospel.* Downers Grove: InterVarsity Press, 2003.

———. *Psalms.* Baker Commentary on the Old Testament. Grand Rapids: Baker Academic, 2006.

———. *Old Testament Theology, Volume Three: Israel's Life.* Downers Grove: InterVarsity Press, 2009.

———. *1 and 2 Samuel for Everyone: A Theological Commentary on the Bible.* Louisville: Westminster John Knox Press, 2011.

———. *Isaiah 56–66 (ICC): A Critical and Exegetical Commentary.* London: Bloomsbury Publishing, 2014.

———. *An Introduction to the Old Testament: Exploring Text, Approaches and Issues.* London: SPCK, 2016.

Graybill, Rhiannon, John Kaltner, and Steven L. McKenzie. *Jonah: A New Translation with Introduction and Commentary.* New Haven: Yale University Press, 2023.

Grice, H. P. "Logic and Conversation." In *Syntax and Semantics, Vol. 3: Speech Acts,* edited by P. Cole and J. Morgan, 41–58. New York: Academic Press, 1975.

———. "Meaning." In *Philosophy of Language: The Big Questions,* edited by Andrea Nye, 118–25. Malden, MA: Blackwell, 1998.

Hartley, John. *Genesis.* Peabody: Hendrickson, 2000.

Havea, Jione. "Numbing Numbers: Land and People of the Wilderness." In *Postcolonial Commentary and the Old Testament,* edited by Hemchand Gossai, 57–69. London: T&T Clark, 2018.

Hill, Andrew and John Walton. *A Survey of the Old Testament,* 2nd ed. Grand Rapids: Zondervan, 2000.

Holbert, John C. "'Deliverance Belongs to Yahweh!' Satire in the Book of Jonah." *Journal for the Study of the Old Testament* 21 (1981): 59–81.

Holroyd, Kristofer. *A S(Word) against Babylon: An Examination of the Multiple Speech Act Layers within Jeremiah 50–51.* Winona Lake: Eisenbrauns, 2017.

Houston, Walter J. "What Did the Prophets Think They Were Doing? Speech Acts and Prophetic Discourse in the Old Testament." *Biblical Interpretation* 1 (1993): 167–88.

Korpel, Marjo C. A. and Johannes C. de Moor. *Adam, Eve, and the Devil: A New Beginning.* Sheffield: Sheffield Phoenix Press, 2014.

Lacocque, André and Pierre-Emmanuel Lacocque. *The Jonah Complex.* Atlanta: John Knox Press, 1981.

Landes, George M. "The Kerygma of the Book of Jonah: The Contextual Interpretation of the Jonah Psalm." *Interpretation* 21 (1967): 3–31.

———. "Review of *Jonah: A New Translation with Introduction, Commentary, and Interpretation,* by Jack M. Sasson, and *Jonah: A Psycho-Religious Approach to the Prophet,* by André Lacocque and Pierre-Emmanuel Lacocque." *Journal of Biblical Literature* 111, no. 1 (1992): 130–34.

Limburg, James. *Jonah.* Louisville: Westminster John Knox Press, 1993.

Lohr, Joel N. "Genesis 4:1-16 in the Masoretic Text, the Septuagint, and the New Testament." *Catholic Biblical Quarterly* 71 (2009): 485–96.

Longman III, Tremper. *The Fear of the Lord is Wisdom: A Theological Introduction to Wisdom in Israel.* Grand Rapids: Baker Academic, 2017.

Lundbom, Jack R. "Parataxis, Rhetorical Structure, and the Dialogue Over Sodom in Genesis 18." In *The World of Genesis: Persons, Places, Perspectives*, edited by Philip R. Davies and David J. A. Clines, 136–45. Sheffield: Sheffield Academic Press, 1998.

Lundin, Roger, Anthony Thiselton, and Clarence Walhout. *The Responsibility of Hermeneutics.* Grand Rapids: Eerdmans, 1985.

Lyons, William John. *Canon and Exegesis: Canonical Praxis and the Sodom Narrative.* London: Sheffield Academic Press, 2002.

MacDonald, Nathan. "Listening to Abraham—Listening to Yhwh: Divine Justice and Mercy in Genesis 18:16-33." *Catholic Biblical Quarterly* 66 (2004): 25–43.

Mangum, Douglas and Wendy Widder. "Speech Act Theory." In *The Lexham Bible Dictionary,* edited by. John D. Barry, et al. Bellingham, WA: Lexham Press, 2016.

Mann, Steven T. *Run, David, Run! An Investigation of the Theological Speech Acts of David's Departure and Return (2 Samuel 14–20).* Winona Lake: Eisenbrauns, 2013.

———. "Performative Prayers of a Prophet: Investigating the Prayers of Jonah as Speech Acts." *Catholic Biblical Quarterly* 79 (2017): 20–40.

———. "Ask and You Shall Intercede: The Peculiar Perlocutionary Power of Asking God Questions." *Bulletin of Biblical Research* 29, no. 2 (2019): 208–24.

———. "Ask and You Shall Intercede: The Power of a Prayerful Imagination." In *Speaking with God: Probing Old Testament Prayers for Contemporary Significance*, edited by Phillip Camp and Elaine Phillips, 154–71. McMaster Divinity College Press, 2021.

———. "Let There Be Cain: A Clash of Imaginations in Genesis 4." *Journal for the Study of the Old Testament* 46 (2021): 79–95.

Mellish, Kevin J. *1 & 2 Samuel: A Commentary in the Wesleyan Tradition.* Kansas City: Beacon Hill Press, 2012.

Meyers, Carol L., Ross S. Kraemer, and Toni Craven. *Women in Scripture: A Dictionary of Named and Unnamed Women in the Hebrew Bible, the Apocryphal/ Deuterocanonical Books, and the New Testament.* Grand Rapids: Eerdmans, 2000.

Milgrom, Jacob. *Numbers.* Philadelphia: The Jewish Publication Society, 1990.

Miller, Patrick D. *They Cried to the Lord: The Form and Theology of Biblical Prayer.* Minneapolis: Fortress Press, 1994.

Moltmann, Jürgen. *Experiences of God.* Philadelphia: Fortress Press, 1980.

Morrison, Craig E. *2 Samuel.* Collegeville, MN: Liturgical Press, 2013.

Nelson, Richard D. *First and Second Kings.* Louisville: Westminster John Knox Press, 2012.

Niditch, Susan. "Genesis." In *Women's Bible Commentary*, edited by Carol A. Newsom, et al. Louisville: Westminster John Knox Press, 2012.

Olson, Dennis T. *Numbers.* Louisville: Westminster John Knox Press, 2012.

Paul, Shalom M. *Amos.* Minneapolis: Fortress Press, 1991.

Perry, T. A. *The Honeymoon is Over: Jonah's Argument with God.* Peabody, MA: Hendrickson, 2006.

Powell, Mark Allan. *What Is Narrative Criticism?* Minneapolis: Fortress Press, 1990.

———. "Narrative Criticism." In *Hearing the New Testament: Strategies for Interpretation,* edited by Joel B. Green, 240–58. Grand Rapids: Eerdmans, 2010.

Pressler, Carolyn. *Numbers.* Nashville: Abingdon Press, 2017.

Propp, William H. C. *Exodus 19–40.* New York: Doubleday, 2006.

Rad, Gerhard von. *Genesis: A Commentary.* Philadelphia: The Westminster Press, 1972.

Riemann, P. "Am I My Brother's Keeper?" *Interpretation* 24 (1970): 482–91.

Roberts, J. J. M. *The Bible and the Ancient Near East.* Winona Lake: Eisenbrauns, 2002.

Rosenberg, David and Harold Bloom. *The Book of J.* New York: Grove Weidenfeld, 1990.

Sakenfeld, Katharine Doob. *Numbers: Journeying with God.* Grand Rapids: Eerdmans, 1995.

Sarna, Nahum M. *Genesis: The Traditional Hebrew Text with the New JPS Translation Commentary.* Philadelphia: The Jewish Publication Society, 1989.

———. *Exodus.* Philadelphia: Jewish Publication Society, 1991.

Sasson, Jack. *Jonah: A New Translation with Introduction, Commentary, and Interpretation.* New York: Doubleday, 1990.

Schneider, Tammi J. *Mothers of Promise: Women in the Book of Genesis.* Grand Rapids: Baker Academic, 2008.

Schüngel-Straumann, Helen. "Genesis 1–11: The Primordial History." In *Feminist Biblical Interpretation: A Compendium of Critical Commentary on the Books of the Bible and Related Literature,* edited by Luise Schottroff and Marie-Theres Wacker, 1–14. Grand Rapids: Eerdmans, 2012.

Searle, John. *Speech Acts: An Essay in the Philosophy of Language.* London: Cambridge University Press, 1969.

———. *Expression and Meaning: Studies in the Theory of Speech Acts.* New York: Cambridge University Press, 1979.

Simon, Uriel. *Jonah.* Philadelphia: Jewish Publication Society, 1999.

Stuart, Douglas. *Hosea–Jonah.* Nashville: Thomas Nelson, 1987.

Swanson, James. *Dictionary of Biblical Languages with Semantic Domains: Hebrew (Old Testament).* Oak Harbor: Logos Research Systems, Inc., 1997.

Trible, Phyllis. *Rhetorical Criticism: Content, Method, and the Book of Jonah.* Minneapolis: Fortress Press, 1994.

Van Seters, John. *Prologue to History: The Yahwist as Historian in Genesis.* Louisville: Westminster John Knox Press, 1992.

Vermeulen, Karolien. "Mind the Gap: Ambiguity in the Story of Cain and Abel." *Journal of Biblical Literature* 133 (2014): 29–42.

Watterson, Bill. *The Calvin and Hobbes Tenth Anniversary Book.* Kansas City: Andrews and McMeel, 1995.

Wenham, Gordon J. *Numbers: An Introduction and Commentary.* Downers Grove: Inter-Varsity Press, 1981.

———. *Genesis 1-15.* Waco: Word Books, 1987.

———. *Story as Torah: Reading Old Testament Narrative Ethically.* Grand Rapids: Baker Academic, 2000.

Westermann, Claus. *The Psalms: Structure, Content & Message.* Translated by Ralph D. Gehrke. Minneapolis: Augsburg Publishing House, 1980.

———. *Genesis 1-11: A Commentary.* Translated by John J. Scullion. Minneapolis: Augsburg Publishing House, 1984.

Wijk-Bos, Johanna W. H. van. *The Road to Kingship: 1-2 Samuel.* Grand Rapids: Eerdmans, 2020.

Wolpe, David. *David: The Divided Heart.* New Haven: Yale University Press, 2014.

Wolterstorff, Nicholas. "Living within a Text." In *Faith and Narrative,* edited by Keith E. Yandell, 202–13. Oxford: Oxford University Press, 2001.

Index

Page references for figures are italicized

Abel, 11, 14–17, 19–20, 22–23
Abraham, 6, 19, 24, 29–35, 37–40, 47, 51, 54–55, 67–68, 105–6
Adah, 20–22
Adam, 12–13, 20, 23
Amos, 6, 29, 34, 37–40, 82, 105–6
Austin, John L. *See* speech act theory, purpose

brother, 15–20, 23
Brueggemann, Walter, 6, 9n24, 33, 51–52, 66–67, 70, 72n11, 76, 84

Cain, 3, 6, 11–24, 26n17, 105–6; mark of, 19, 27n31
Caleb, 61–66, 68, *69*
chiasm, 22, 31–33, *32*, 64, 68, *69*, 70, 87, *89*, 89–95, *91*, 101n14
colonialism, 67–68
commitment (/חֶסֶד), 7, 65–67, 69, 72n18, 75, 78, *79*, 80, 87, *91*, 91–94, *96*, 96–98, 100, 102n28
covenant, 7, 31, 33, 35–39, 51–52, 55, 59, 67, 75, 83, 85, 94, 102n28
curse, *16*, 17–18, 27n35

David, 7, 52–53, 75–78, *79*, 80–85, 86n12, 106
Deborah, 21

Egypt/Egyptians, 4, *35*, 35–36, 38, 45, *46*, 46–52, *48*, 55, *63*, 63–65, 67–68, *69*, 71, *77*, 105
Enoch, 20
Enosh, 24
Eve, 6, 11–13, 20, 23–24, 105–6

fear of God, 7, 45, *46*, 49, 54–55, 57n19, 106
Frymer-Kensky, Tikva, 50, 52, 56n4

Gafney, Wilda C., 50, 52, 56n1
God: accessibility of, 75, 81, 84; change of mind, 30–31, 37–38, 42n27, 95–96, 98; commitment of. *See* commitment (/חֶסֶד); compassion of, 38, 99; deliverance of, 89, 92, 99–100; forgiveness of, 38–39, 59, 65, 69–71; freedom of, 84, 106; glory of, 65–66; grace of, 13, 29, 34, 37, 40, 106; holiness of, 33;

immutability of, 36; judgment of,
31, 33, 37–38, 40, 42n29, 64–66,
70, 98–99, 101; justice of, 30, 31,
31–32, 33–34, 38; military name, 78;
omniscience of, 36; partnership with
Eve, 12–13; punishment of, 7, *18*,
18, 19, 20, 34, 38–39, 59, 66, 68, 70,
71, 97; relationship with David, 78,
80; relationship with humanity, 24,
30, 40, 98, 105–6; relationship with
Israel, 38, 59, 63, 66–67, 69, 71, 75,
85, 98; relationship with the king,
83, 85; reputation of, 33, 36–38, 65,
69; self-identification of, 65, 69, 96;
tendency to side with the weak, 38;
wrath of, 34–35, *35*, 106
golden calf, 34, 36, 65
Goldingay, John, 5, 42n19, 68, 70,
83–84, 86n17, 92
Gomorrah, 31, 34, 39

hermeneutics, biblical, 2, 8n7, 83;
hermeneutic of self-involvement, 87,
93–95, 99–100

idolatry, 36
imagine/imaginary/imagination, 5–7,
11–15, 18, 20–24, 29, 32–38, 40,
41n4, 45, 47–49, 51–52, 55, 59–60,
63–65, 71, 75, 77–78, 81, 84–85,
105–7
immigrant, 20
intercession/intercessory prayer, 6,
29–31, *30*, 33–40, 45, 59, 65–66, 68,
69, 70–71, 105–6
Israel/Israelites, 7, 20, 34–35, *35*,
36–39, 46, *47*, 47–48, 50–52, 54–55,
56n1, 59–68, *64*, *69*, 70–71, 72n11,
75, *77*, 77–78, *79*, 80–83, 85, 98, 105

Jael, 53
Jericho, king of, 52, *53*
Jeroboam, 42–43n29, 82, 86n15
Jesus, 40, 83
Jezebel, 56n1

Job, 54, 92
Jonah, 7, 42n25, 87–100, *89*, *91*, 101n7,
102n41, 106
Joseph, 42n26, 46, 51
Joshua, 64–66, 68, *69*

kingdom, 37, 39, 78, *79*, 80, 82;
kingdom of God, 83
kinsman redeemer, 18

Lamech, 6, 11, 20–21, *21*, 22–24, 105–6
land, 7, *16*, *18*, 19, 30, *31*, *32*, 33, *37*,
47, 47, *53*, 59–68, *61–64*, *69*, 70–71,
72n11, *79*, 82, *89*, 93, 105

Michal, 52–53
midwives, 4–5, 7, 45, *46*, *48*, 48–52,
54–55, 56n4, 106
Miriam, 21
monarchy, 83, 86n17
Moses, 6–7, 29, 34–40, *35*, 45, *46*,
51–52, 55, 59–60, 63, 67–68, *69*,
70–71, 72n18, 84, 105–6

Nathan, 76–78, 80–81, 84–85
neighbor, neighborliness, 20, 51, 67
Nephilim, 62
Nineveh, 7, 95–99, 101n12

parallelism, 15, 17, 20
patriarchy, 12–13, 24
Pharaoh, 4–5, 7, 38, 45, *46*, 47–52,
54–55, 84, 105–6
prayer, 6–7, 29, *30*, 33–35, 37–40,
45, 80, 87–100, *89*, 105–6; prayer,
intercessory. *See also* intercession/
intercessory prayer
psalms/Psalms/Psalter, 9n24, 21, 33, 34,
37, 70, 88, 91–95, 99
Puah. *See* midwives

question(s), 2, 6–7, 14–17, 19–21,
27n22, 29–30, *30–32*, 32–36, *35*,
38–40, 47, 49–50, 60, 76–78, 83,

85, 88, 91–92, 96–97, 99–100;
    rhetorical, 17–19, 41n15, 102n41

Rahab, 52, *53*
repent, repentance, 17, 37–38, 40, 92,
    97–99
righteous/righteousness, 30–35, *31*, *32*,
    39, 40, 41n12, 42n15

Sarah, 67, 70
Saul, 52–53, *79*, 80
Seth, 11, 23–24
Shiphrah. *See* midwives
sin, 3, 11, *14*, 15–16, 18, 20, 24, 26n18,
    27n28, 31–32, 36, 39–40, 65, 69, 92,
    97, 105
Sisera, 53
Sodom, *30*, 30–32, *32*, 33–35, 39, 41n9
Solomon, 81–84, 86n14
speech act theory: direction of fit, 3–6;
    distinction between illocutionary and
    perlocutionary acts, 2–3; purpose, 2;
    sincerity condition, 3–4; taxonomy
    of illocutionary acts, 3–4
spies, 7, 52, 59–60, *62*, 62–64, 66, 68,
    69, 71, 105–6

status quo, 51
story and storyteller level, distinction
    between, 5–6

tabernacle, 77, *77*, 81
temple, 7, 75–78, 80–85, 86n15, *89*,
    91–92, 94, 106
Torah, 20, 55, 67
totalism, 54
Trible, Phyllis, 90, 93, 101n14, 101n23

victim, 20, 53
villain, 1, 11, 81
violent/violence, 6, 11, 15, 18, 20–24,
    34, 48, 105

wilderness, 39, *63*, 66–67, *69*, 70–71,
    71
van Wijk-Bos, Johanna W. H., 76, 78,
    80–81
wisdom, 47, 51, 54
women, 45, 49, 52–53, 55

Zillah, 20–22, *21*

About the Author

Steven T. Mann (PhD, Fuller Theological Seminary) is an associate professor of biblical and theological studies at Azusa Pacific Seminary, Azusa Pacific University, and author of *Run, David, Run! An Investigation of the Theological Speech Acts of David's Departure and Return (2 Samuel 14–20)* from Eisenbrauns/Penn State University Press.